BATHROOM BOOK
of
MANITOBA TRIVIA
Weird, Wacky and Wild

Lisa Wojna

BLU
BL
BOO

The Publisher: Blue Bike Books

Website: www.bluebikebooks.com

Library and Archives Canada Cataloguing in Publication

Wojna, Lisa, 1962–   Bathroom book of Manitoba trivia : weird, wacky
    and wild / Lisa Wojna.

(Bathroom books of Canada; 12)

ISBN-13: 978-1-897278-28-4
ISBN-10: 1-897278-28-4

    1. Manitoba—Miscellanea. I. Title.
FC3361.W65 2007   971.27   C2007-901523-9

Project Director: Nicholle Carrière
Project Editor: Erin McCloskey
Production: Michael Cooke
Cover Image: Roger Garcia
Illustrations: Patrick Henaff, Roger Garcia, Graham Johnson

We acknowledge the support of the Alberta Foundation for the Arts for our
publishing program.

PC: P5

DEDICATION

To Dominik Wojna and Peter Stadnyk. Foresight or happen-
stance, whatever led these two men to settle in Manitoba makes
my heart sing with appreciation.

ACKNOWLEDGEMENTS

I've always maintained that while writing may be a solitary
occupation, putting a book together certainly is not. My most
sincere gratitude goes out to several folks who helped in putting
this project together. As always, thank you to dear Faye, friend
and mentor. Thank you to Erin, my editor. My most sincere
appreciation for the sharp mind and eagle eye needed to fine
tune this document and order and reorder sections until they
flowed just perfectly. Thanks to all the folks in Manitoba who
received my cold calls for information or clarification and
responded with the traditionally cheery disposition that people
in the province are so well known for. And a heartfelt thanks to
my family—Garry, Peter, Melissa, Matthew, Nathan and Jada.
Without their support I'd still be staring at a blank page.

CONTENTS

INTRODUCTION

I frequently explain to people that, as a youngster who was born and raised surrounded by fields on the outskirts of Winnipeg, I always dreamed of living just about anywhere else in the universe. My imagination was fuelled by Sunday Cinema movies such as *Heidi*. Oh! To live in the Swiss Alps, spending my days strolling along the rolling hillsides, wind whispering through my hair, my faithful dog by my side, my lungs filling with pure alpine air, was just one of many dreams.

There was also the television-land fantasy of *Lassie*, *Batman*, *Bewitched*, even the *Brady Bunch*; whether the story setting was a rustic farm, a gothic darkness or a simple city suburb, I longed to escape the airy nothingness I perceived around me and go there—go anywhere. Blame it on being young and adventurous or just plain immature. Blame it on job opportunities. Blame it on the economy. Blame it on the rain. Blame it on whatever you like, all I could think of was getting out and moving on.

So just before Christmas 1994, my family and I pulled up stakes and moved to the wilds of northern British Columbia. We had known about our move since September and had planned meticulously. "Just think," one writer friend of mine said to me. "How inspiring it will be to sit in your study, look out your window and see nothing but mountain wilderness." Yeah, I'd be inspired. In fact, I had visions of becoming the next Canadian literary firecracker. Move over Arnason. Stand back Kroesch. This experience was all I needed to make my mark.

Thrilled by my newfound confidence and eager to take a bite out of the Canadian *literati*, I was so organized that my family was living out of boxes for many weeks before our possessions were eventually loaded on the moving van and bound for BC. I was excited. I was inspired—until the day we pulled out of our driveway and pointed our dusty Dodge Caravan westward. That oh-so-cliché lump formed in my throat, and I knew I was making a mistake. I was immediately homesick.

Northern BC was wild and wonderful in many ways, and during my time there I believe that I grew as a writer but even more so as an individual. I managed to ditch an old spouse and pick up a new one. Still, the prairie would not cease in calling me, so I took one step closer to home and moved to Alberta at the dawn of the new millennium. This move would provide yet another interesting experience (I now have a clearer understanding of the term "redneck"), but at least I was in the prairies. These days my summers are spent making cursory visits to BC (for that new husband I picked up) and lengthy visits back home to Manitoba. Rather than motoring down to Arizona for winter or hiding out in Victoria (it's going to drop off into the ocean someday anyway), I hope to spend at least a few of my "golden years" living back home. In the meantime, although I still dream of writing that great Canadian novel, I'm thrilled with the opportunity to write this book of trivia. Manitoba was my birth home, and Manitoba is the home of my heart. It's more than just a great place to be from; it's a great place to live.

FRIENDLY MANITOBA

Much More Than Prairie

Folks driving across the province on the Trans-Canada Highway (or Highway 1) might wonder if Manitoba indeed has a "wow factor." This arrow-straight portion of road ploughs through some of the most pancake-flat portions of the province, rivalling even Saskatchewan for having the most exciting noticeable landmark in sight being a fence post and some barbed wire. But have a "wow factor" Manitoba definitely does. In fact, it has several.

One of Manitoba's biggest "wow factors" is its abundance of freshwater. Known as the "land of 100,000 lakes," Manitoba offers its residents the best in summer recreation. Whiteshell Provincial Park, where I like to spend my summers, consists of a chain of lake communities along the Ontario border that are interconnected through the Winnipeg River system. North of Winnipeg are three large freshwater lakes—Lake Winnipeg, Lake Manitoba and Lake Winnipegosis. The beaches of these three lakes have drawn avid sunbathers and sports enthusiasts alike for as long as folks here can remember. Of course, the northeastern portion of the province nestles along the shores of Hudson Bay, which, together with neighbouring James Bay, makes up one of the world's largest seas. The ecosystems and natural habitats formed around these lakes and bays and the 263,000 square kilometres of forests covering the province, along with many other natural attributes, make Manitoba a nature-lover's dream.

People are another Manitoba "wow factor." Between 1881 and 1918, the city of Winnipeg was known as the "Chicago of the North" and one of North America's fastest growing cities. With that growth came unprecedented immigration, and what began as little more than a small colony of settlers gathered on the junction of the Red and Assiniboine rivers grew into a thriving city in a province that regards itself as "one of the most ethnically diverse provinces in Canada." Along with the 100 languages spoken among the vast number of ethnic groups, Manitoba is for all intents and purposes (though not officially) bilingual. Even many street signs are in English and French. Every summer Winnipeg salutes its rich cultural mosaic with Folklorama, a two-week long multicultural festival like none other in the country. If you needed further proof of its commitment to its people, just take a look at its licence plates that, since 1976, have boasted "Friendly Manitoba."

With some of the most varied natural environments in the country and absolutely the nicest people around, I dare you to take a second look at this frequently overlooked province.

Wow.

SYMBOLS AND SIGNIFICANCES

Naming a Province

How a place gets its name is often shrouded in mystery—or at the very least a little uncertainty—and Manitoba is no exception. That the name was derived from the language of Manitoba's Native peoples is an agreed-upon fact among scholars and historians, but there are several theories as to its evolution. One school of thought credits the Cree Nation, referring to their words *Manitou*, meaning "great spirit," and *wapow* or "narrows." Another credits the similar Ojibwe term *Manitou-bau* (or *baw*). Both phrases refer to "the narrows of Lake Manitoba" and the sound of wind and water crashing on the shoreline, which, for some First Nations peoples, represented the voice or drumbeat of the *Manitou* or Great Spirit. The Assiniboine people also have a unique phrase that some believe may have played a role in the development of the province's name. In their language, *mine* (water) and *toba* (prairies) combine to form "lake of the prairies."

Political leader Thomas Spence is thought to be the first non-Native to refer to the area around his Portage la Prairie–area settlement as Manitoba in 1858. But it wasn't until May 1870 when Sir John A. Macdonald made it official when he declared the province of Manitoba was entering Confederation and explained the name was chosen "for its pleasant sound and its associations with the original inhabitants of the area." On July 15, 1870, it was a done deal.

DID YOU KNOW?

The Cree had given the name *Win-nipi* (murky waters) to what is now known as Lake Winnipeg, one of three large freshwater lakes north of Manitoba's capital city, also named Winnipeg.

Also Known As

Manitoba seems to have acquired a selection of nicknames throughout its over 137 years of history. Here are a few:

- ☛ The Postage Stamp Province: This one dates back to the early years of the province when its first boundaries measured 208 kilometres east to west and 176 kilometres north to south (or, as was recorded at the time, 130 by 110 miles). The nice, compact package looked a little like a postage stamp, hence the name.

- ☛ The Bull's Eye of the Dominion: Simply put, Manitoba is located in the geographic centre of the country. A "bull's eye," so to speak.

- ☛ The Gateway to the West: Again, this is in reference to its central location. Anything west of Manitoba is, of course, western Canada. However, because most Manitobans consider themselves westerners, the "gateway" is thought by most Manitobans to refer to the Manitoba–Ontario border.

- ☛ Sunny Manitoba: With an average of 2377 hours of sunlight expected each year the reasons for this nickname need no explanation.

- ☛ Land of 100,000 Lakes: Thanks to Lake Agassiz, which following the last ice age covered a good portion of the province, Manitoba actually has more than 100,000 lakes according to its government website.

- ☛ The Keystone Province: This one is courtesy of Lord Dufferin who, in 1877, said, "Manitoba may be regarded as the keystone of that mighty arch of sister provinces which spans the continent." Consequently, Manitobans have come to regard their province as "the one that holds the nation together."

Mark My Words
Manitoba's motto is simple and strong—"Glorious and Free."

Flying High

It may have been the fifth province to enter Confederation back in 1870, but it wasn't until almost 100 years later, on May 12, 1966, when Manitoba officially had a flag of its own. The flag is predominantly fire-engine red with a Union Jack prominently displayed on the upper left corner and the provincial shield on the centre right.

Manitoba's Mystery

The Manitoba provincial shield plays a significant role in both the province's flag and its coat of arms. The lower two-thirds portion of the shield features a bison perched on a rocky foundation with a kelly green background; the top third displays the red cross of St. George (a prominent symbol of Canada's British heritage). While the shield was officially adopted in 1905, just who designed this Manitoba emblem is unknown.

Armorial Bearings

Manitoba's coat of arms was first adopted by King Edward VII on May 10, 1905. The provincial shield occupies centre stage, flanked by a unicorn to the left and a white horse to the right. A helmet crowns the shield, the beaver (Canada's national animal) sits atop the helmet while holding a crocus (Manitoba's official floral emblem) and wearing a crown to signify royal sovereignty. The entire lot sits on a base covered with wheat, crocuses and spruce, to represent the landscape, and a wave of blue, to represent water. Underscoring it all is written *Gloriosus et Liber*, meaning "Glorious and Free."

Wise and Wonderful

It took considerable debate among naturalists, school groups and the general public before the great grey owl was officially chosen as Manitoba's provincial bird on July 16, 1987. The stately bird is the largest owl in North America and lives in wooded areas throughout the province.

Beauty in Blue

School children were also heavily involved in choosing this provincial symbol, and on March 16, 1906, *Anemone patens*—also affectionately known as the prairie crocus—was officially adopted as Manitoba's official floral emblem.

Tall and Strong

Everything about the white spruce made it a good choice as Manitoba's official provincial tree. Its lumber was used to help build this nation's towns and cities. It grows throughout the province. It's strong, beautiful and disease resistant—and it makes a great Christmas tree besides. What more could anyone ask for in a tree?

Coat of Many Colours

The Manitoba tartan is more than just a piece of cloth; it's a reflection of the tapestry of life that makes up this wonderfully diverse province. Officially adopted on May 1, 1962, each colour woven through this unique design was chosen for a specific reason. The dark red squares represent the province's natural resources, the azure blue lines stand for Winnipeg's founder Lord Selkirk, the gold lines signify Manitoba's mark as an agricultural producer and the dark green lines exemplify the province's multicultural flavour.

DID YOU KNOW?

Manitoba has a multiculturalism emblem. The design, an intricate diamond-shaped logo made up of nine independent yet interlocking diamonds, stands as a symbol of cross-cultural harmony and co-operation.

Biggest and Best

One of Manitoba's best-known symbols is the Golden Boy. Perched high on the dome of Manitoba's provincial building located in downtown Winnipeg, the 5.25-metre-tall, gilded bronze statue of a boy holds a sheaf of wheat in his left arm and torch in his right hand. Sculpted by Parisian artist Charles Gardet in 1918, the statue is said to represent the spirit of enterprise and eternal youth.

The Golden Boy had an adventurous beginning. First, the French foundry where it was being cast was partly destroyed in World War I. Then the Golden Boy's journey to Canada was interrupted—the grain ship it was stowed on was seconded to transport troops. Thankfully, it arrived safely and was secured in place on time for the official opening of the provincial building in 1920. There it remains as a proud symbol for all Manitobans.

THE WONDERS OF WINNIPEG

Just the Facts

☛ Winnipeg comes from the Cree word *win-nipi*, meaning "muddy" or "murky waters"

☛ The city was incorporated on November 8, 1873

☛ According to a 2005 census estimate, 706,900 people call Winnipeg home

☛ Population-wise, Winnipeg is the country's ninth largest city

☛ Winnipeg has two nicknames: "The Peg" and "Winterpeg." It's also known as "the windy city."

☛ Its motto is *Unum Cum Virtute Multorum* or "One With The Strength of Many"

☛ Eight Members of Parliament and 31 members of a legislative assembly originally hail from the city

ARCHITECTURE

A History in Wood and Stone

Tour the core of downtown Winnipeg, and if you didn't have an appreciation for heritage buildings, you'll likely get one. By March 2006, a report by Winnipeg's Planning, Property and Development Department cited 220 buildings that had been placed on the city's conservation list. From humble homes and Winnipeg's first mansions to heritage churches and the neo-gothic majesty of buildings such as the Hotel Fort Garry, the boom experienced by the city's early years paved the way for a community rich in architecture. On September 27, 1997, the Canadian government officially recognized the Exchange District in the downtown core when the federal Minister of Canadian Heritage declared the area a National Historic Site.

Sky High

Before 1920, Winnipeg already boasted as many as 14 skyscrapers.

Oldest and Best

The St. Boniface Museum is housed in the former Grey Nun convent on Tache Avenue. Built between 1845 and 1851, the museum is Winnipeg's oldest building and North America's largest oak log structure.

Bad Luck Basilica

Built in 1818, the St. Boniface Basilica Cathedral represented strength of spirit and faith to the area's new settlers. It was built by Father Provencher, who replaced the first structure with a second cathedral in 1832. Tragedy struck in 1860 when the second cathedral was consumed by fire. Archbishop Taché saw to the building of a smaller third cathedral, and the faithful of the area made do with this structure until 1908 when a yet a fourth cathedral was built. This one was bigger and more magnificent than its predecessors and was considered the best example of French Romanesque architecture in Manitoba. It, too, would have a relatively short-lived existence. On July 22, 1968, often referred to by the faithful as "Black Monday," fire ravaged the fourth building as well. Like a phoenix rising from the ashes, a fifth cathedral rose up from the ruins of its predecessor. The new structure is literally overshadowed by portions of the sacristy, facade and walls that remain of the former Basilica.

DID YOU  KNOW?

The remains of six bishops and four missionaries are entombed in the crypt of St. Boniface Basilica Cathedral. The cathedral is also home to the largest and oldest Catholic cemetery in western Canada and is the final resting place of the Father of Manitoba, Louis Riel.

CLIMATE

Four Very Distinct Seasons

Manitoba is a province with four true seasons. Here, April showers do bring May flowers, summer means mosquito-producing heat waves, and autumn colours reign long and luxurious until a mean winter hits and locks in for weeks on end. While average temperatures in July and August are around 25°C, it's not uncommon for them to soar into the high 30s. Similarly, winter temperatures are almost always below freezing and average around –20°C, but they can dip far lower and even remain, for weeks at a time, in the –30s.

Just a Sample

Location	Average January Temp. (Celsius)	Average July Temp. (Celsius)
Brandon	–18.4°	+18°
Thompson	–25°	+15.7°
Churchill	–26.9°	+11.8°
Winnipeg	–20°	+24.7°

Extreme Extremes

(Source: Environment Canada)

☛ Southern Manitoba was hit with a series of tornadoes on June 22, 1922, killing five people, injuring hundreds more and causing an estimated $2 million in damages.

☛ In 1933, the prairies had just emerged from the fall-out of the 1929 stock market crash and were almost immediately faced with a demon of a different kind. Warm, dry weather throughout that summer left farmers scrambling for ways to water their livestock and revive dying crops. By harvest time the message was clear—there was no harvest. Hardy folk that farmers are, they started planning for the next year. What followed, however, were four more years of drought caused by an average rainfall that missed normal levels by as much as 60 percent, giving the era the dubious distinctions of the "Dustbowl Era" and the "Dirty Thirties."

☛ During the Dustbowl Era, Manitoba and Ontario experienced their longest, deadliest heat wave on record. From July 5 to 17, 1936, temperatures soared as high as 44°C. The heat claimed 1180 lives between the two provinces.

☛ The blizzard of 1947, which spanned the three Prairie Provinces and lasted from January 30 to February 8, made it into the annals of weather trivia as the worst blizzard in Canadian history because some roads and railway tracks in neighbouring Saskatchewan were blocked until spring. Some folks reported having to dig man-sized tunnels just to make it to their outhouses.

☛ One death was reported after the Red River overflowed its bank in 1950, flooding Winnipeg streets for up to six weeks. An eighth of the city was under water and an estimated $550 million in property damages were reported.

☛ The year was 1966, and although I was only four years old, I remember this monumental Winnipeg snowstorm. March 4 received a record snowfall of 35 centimetres (or 13.75 inches, since back then Canadians were still measuring imperial style). Mayor Stephen Juba issued a citywide warning, encouraging residents to stay home.

☛ Chicken Little would relate to this. Farmers cringe at the thought of golf-ball-sized hail pummelling their crops. Imagine the reaction of Winnipeg-area farmers on July 24, 1996, when hail the size of oranges fell from the sky. A similar storm hit Calgary the same day, and between the two cities about $300 million in damages was reported.

☞ In the Red River Flood of 1950, the river crested at 9.2 metres (30 feet) above normal near Winnipeg, setting a record for the day—but not in a good way. During his rein as premier, from 1958 to 1967, Duff Roblin took a lot of heat for pushing ahead with building a floodway to prevent the kind of destruction that took place during the 1950 flood. If the 17 times it had been utilized since its completion in 1968 didn't calm the critics, any doubts as to the usefulness of Duff's Ditch, as it became affectionately known, were put to rest in April and May 1997. At its peak that year, even with the floodway, the river crested 12 metres above normal, causing half a billion dollars in damages. What would have happened without Duff's Ditch?

GEOGRAPHY

Many Roles

Manitoba can be thought to occupy three roles: a gateway to the west, a gateway to the east and the geographic centre of the country.

Varied Landscape

While wheat fields and other crops stretch as far as the eye can see, Manitoba is more than the flat-as-a-pancake image many outsiders have of the province. In fact, almost half of the province—263,000 square kilometres—is made up of coniferous and deciduous forest. Another 14 percent is water. So, away with the misconceptions.

Neighbours

The province is flanked by Saskatchewan to the west and Ontario to the east. Its northern border is shared between the territory of Nunavut and Hudson Bay. To the south, Manitoba borders the American states of Minnesota and North Dakota.

Region by Region

Simply put, the province can be divided into eight main regions: Northern, Central Plains, Eastman, Westman, Pembina Valley, Interlake, Parkland and Winnipeg Capital Region—by name alone one gets a fairly good idea where they might be located. The Central Plains region is located around the longitudinal centre of the province, Portage la Prairie. The Eastman region is tucked away in the southeastern portion of the province, the Westman region is the southwestern corner and the Pembina Valley is flanked by Westman and Eastman. The Interlake region is nestled between the southern portions of Lake Winnipeg and Lake Manitoba. The Parkland region takes in

Dauphin, Riding Mountain National Park and the surrounding area, while the Winnipeg Capital Region, of course, surrounds Winnipeg. These seven regions occupy only the bottom quarter of the province. The remaining portion is the Northern region.

Surf and Turf

Manitoba is ranked the country's eighth largest province, covering a total area of 649,950 square kilometres. Of that, 548,360 square kilometres is land and 14 percent, or 101,593 square kilometres, is water.

Comparatively Speaking

Lake Winnipeg is the 10th largest fresh water lake in the world.

DID YOU KNOW?

Manitoba started out as a little square, measuring 208 kilometres east to west and 176 kilometres north to south (130 miles by 110 miles) when it entered Confederation and became a province on July 15, 1870. Those boundaries were extended twice, once in 1881 and again in 1912, defining the provincial border as it is today.

Long and Lean

At its widest point, about two-thirds of the way north, Manitoba measures 793 kilometres across. However, the measurements of the province's width at its northern and southernmost points are very similar at 418 kilometres and 449 kilometres respectively. Travel as the crow flies from the Manitoba–U.S. boundary in the south to the province's northern tip to cover 1225 kilometres.

Prehistoric Beginnings

A portion of central southwestern Manitoba is historically tied to parts of southwestern Ontario, northwestern Minnesota and northeastern North Dakota. During the Pleistocene epoch, (estimated between 1,808,000 to 11,550 BCE), a lake larger than all the Great Lakes combined occupied a portion of land in this area measuring 1130 kilometres in length and 400 kilometres in width or an estimated 440,000 square kilometres. Known as Lake Agassiz, throughout the years it drained in various directions: into the Minnesota River, the Great Lakes or even into Yukon Territory and Alaska. The largest remnant of this mammoth lake is Lake Winnipeg.

DID YOU KNOW?

At its largest, Lake Agassiz was bigger than any lake in the world today and may have even rivalled the Caspian Sea in size.

Heaven Sent

The central part of Manitoba's deepest lake, with depths measuring 115 metres, was caused by the impact of a meteor colliding with Earth. West Hawk Lake is located in the Whiteshell Provincial Park just a few miles from the Ontario border. Geologists estimate the collision forming the lake's central crater, which has a diameter of about 2.4 kilometres, was formed about 100 million years ago.

Ancient Art

Tour around the granite cliffs that surround a large portion of West Hawk Lake and chances are you'll come upon a petroform or two. Petroforms are shapes of turtles, snakes, humans or other patterns formed on granite rock using granite boulders. West Hawk Lake is just one of a number of locations in the Whiteshell where petroforms can be found.

Manitoba's Rivers

There are about 43 rivers spiderwebbing their way across the province.

- ☛ The Assiniboine River runs for about 1070 kilometres, flowing through Saskatchewan and meeting up with the Red River near the Forks.

- ☛ For 877 kilometres, the Red River flows north, forming a natural border between Minnesota and North Dakota, and makes its way throughout the Red River Valley to Lake Winnipeg's Netley Marsh.

- ☛ The Winnipeg River system snakes along the Ontario border and into the heart of the province for 813 kilometres from Lake of the Woods to Lake Winnipeg, feeding a succession of natural lakes in its path.

- ☛ Flowing eastward and draining in Lake Winnipeg, the Saskatchewan River traverses about 550 kilometres.

DID YOU KNOW?

At some point, most Manitoba rivers flow north and empty into the Hudson Bay.

TREASURED WILDLIFE

Room to Roam

Spend a little time to really travel throughout the province and you'll see Manitoba's landscape is rich and varied, providing prime habitat to a great many plant, animal and bird species. But as in many parts of the world, human encroachment is limiting natural habitat and damaging land. The grizzly bear once roamed the province freely and in solid numbers. Today, it is listed on Manitoba Conservation's extirpated list—animals that no longer inhabit their traditional range and if they exist at all are likely in captivity. Other species on this list are:

- greater prairie chicken
- long-billed curlew
- trumpeter swan
- Riding's satyr butterfly
- musk ox
- pronghorn sheep
- swift fox

Sounding the Trumpet

The trumpeter swan is North America's largest waterfowl. By 1900, this majestic bird was almost extinct, and by 1933 only 66 were thought to be left. The Wetlands Research Station at Delta was the first to begin breeding the trumpeter in captivity, and the birds' numbers have now increased to between 11,000 and 13,000.

DID YOU  KNOW?

The last pronghorn antelope to roam freely in the province was believed to have been shot in 1881 at Whitewater Lake.

Endangered Species

Without planned conservation attempts, the following species are in danger of disappearing from Manitoba's landscape altogether:

- ☞ Baird's sparrow
- ☞ burrowing owl
- ☞ Eskimo curlew
- ☞ loggerhead shrike
- ☞ peregrine falcon
- ☞ piping plover
- ☞ whooping crane
- ☞ Uncas skipper butterfly
- ☞ small white lady's slipper
- ☞ Great Plains ladies' tresses
- ☞ western prairie fringed orchid

Dwindling Numbers

The burrowing owl faces huge challenges to its survival. Its habitat is open grasslands, making it prey for small animals such as the fox. Since farming operations occupy much of the prairie, the owl risks having its nest ploughed over or being poisoned by insecticides and pesticides. In 1990, only 19 nesting pairs were thought to inhabit the province; recent numbers from Manitoba Conservation from 1997 to 2002 state between 0–3 nesting pairs.

Threatened Species

When populations rapidly decline species are said to be "threatened." Without aggressive intervention that status can quickly become "endangered." Here are the species on Manitoba's threatened list:

- ferruginous hawk
- mule deer
- western silvery aster
- western spiderwort
- Culver's root
- Riddell's goldenrod
- Ottoe skipper
- Dakota skipper
- Great Plains toad

Leader of the Pack

The city of Winnipeg gave the world one of the pillars of the national and international environmental movements. Robert Lorne Hunter was born in the city suburb of St. Boniface in 1941 and was well into the environmental movement by age 25 when he became a member of the Don't Make a Wave Committee—a group that protested American underground nuclear testing at a wildlife refuge off the coast of Alaska. Just a few years later, in 1972, he and BC native Patrick Moore founded Greenpeace—an environmental group of international proportions. Perhaps one of Robert's most crowning achievements was his successful campaign to ban commercial whaling. Robert was named "One of the 10 'Eco-Heroes' of the 20th Century" by *Time Magazine*. He died in 2005 at the age of 63.

DID YOU KNOW?

The city of Winnipeg has 4152 hectares of parkland, more parks per capita than any other city in North America.

Most Elusive

Manitoba is not to be excluded when it comes to Sasquatch sightings. Bill Borody, founder of the Manitoba Sasquatch Research Centre located near Anola, has received more than 300 reported sightings in the last 30 years here in this fair province. With a population density of just 1.82 persons per square kilometre, that leaves a lot of room for the large, furry creatures to remain incognito!

THE PEOPLE

The Whole Picture

Based on a recent Statistics Canada estimate, Manitoba's population is 1,180,004. Of that number, more than 648,600 people live in the provincial capital, Winnipeg.

Fits and Starts

(Source: Statistics Canada)

Throughout its history, Manitoba's population has seen a steady increase, moving it in ranking from the eighth most populated province in 1871 to fifth spot today. But there were times when growth sped rapidly, then slipped a little. Here are the numbers.

Year	Population
1871	25,228
1881	62,260
1891	152,506
1901	255,211
1911	461,394
1921	610,118
1931	700,139
1941	729,744
1951	776,541
1961	921,686
1971	988,245
1981	1,026,241
1991	1,091,942
2001	1,119,583
2006	1,177,800

The largest 10-year change occurred between 1871 and 1881, when the provincial population increased 146.8 percent, and between 1901 and 1911 when it increased by 80.8 percent.

Compared With Our Neighbours

The population of Manitoba seems small when compared with a countrywide population of more than 32 million, but looks can be deceiving. While it trails significantly behind Ontario, with more than 12.5 million people, Manitoba is actually the fifth most populated province. Here's the Statistics Canada comparison, based on 2006 numbers:

Province	Population
Ontario	12,687,000
Quebec	7,651,500
British Columbia	4,310,500
Alberta	3,375,800
Manitoba	**1,177,800**
Saskatchewan	985,400
Nova Scotia	934,400
New Brunswick	749,200
Newfoundland and Labrador	509,700
Prince Edward Island	138,500
Northwest Territories	41,900
Yukon Territory	31,200
Nunavut	30,800

The Manitoba Mosaic

As one of Canada's most ethnically diverse provinces, Manitoba's population is a true mosaic. Twenty-nine main ethnic origins were reported, based on 2001 Census information. The highest single response, when it came to identifying ethnic background, was "Canadian." English, German, Scottish, Ukrainian, Irish, French, North American Indian, Polish and Métis, respectively, round out the top 10 responses.

DID YOU KNOW?

Although the Icelandic community in Manitoba accounts for about only 26,500 people (based on the 2001 Census) this number represents the "largest Icelandic population outside of Iceland."

Religious Preferences

The majority of Manitobans consider themselves Christians, with 29 percent Catholic, 43 percent Protestant Christians, one percent Christian Orthodox and four percent "Christian not included elsewhere." Manitoba's diverse ethnic population is also mirrored in the number of faiths practising in the province.

Religion	Number practising
Jewish	13,040
Buddhist	5745
Sikh	5485
Muslim	5095
Hindu	3835
Eastern religions	795
Other religions	4780

About 18 percent of Manitoba's population declared themselves to be without any religious affiliation.

The City Scene

With most of Manitoba's population residing in and around Winnipeg City, one can only wonder how the rest of the province shapes up in comparison (based on 2001 Census data):

Community	Population
Winnipeg	**648,600**
Brandon	39,716
Thompson	13,256
Portage la Prairie	13,077
Churchill	963

First Nations Heritage

The Assembly of Manitoba Chiefs defines five main First Nations ethnicities with distinct territories in the province. They are the Cree, who traditionally occupied the northern part of the province; the Ojibwe, whose traditional lands were in the south; the Dakota, who occupied the southwest; the Dene, in the northwestern corner of the province; and the Ojibwe-Cree, located in the northeast.

A further breakdown of the First Nations population uncovers about 32 individual First Nations groupings in northern Manitoba and about 30 in southern Manitoba.

Statistics Canada's 2001 Census Findings

- ☞ 150,040 of Manitoba's total population of 1,103,700 are of First Nations descent

- ☞ 52,060 of Manitoba's First Nations population live on a reservation and 97,980 live off the reserve

- ☞ 24,980 off-reserve First Nations people live in a rural setting, while 73,105 live in an urban setting

- ☞ 90,340 of Manitoba's First Nations people are listed as North American Indian

- 56,800 of Manitoba's First Nations people are Métis

- 340 of Manitoba's First Nations people are Inuit

- Less than four percent, or 5540 of 145,695 people in Canada, are Native peoples aged 65 years and older

- 25 percent, or 18,000 of 71,030 people in Canada, are Native peoples aged four years and younger

DID YOU KNOW?

The largest population increase in any Manitoba ethnic group occurs with the First Nations peoples. Studies from Indian and Northern Affairs, Canada's Basic Departmental Data points out that between 1978 and 1999, Manitoba's First Nations population had increased 125 percent from 44,642 people in 1978 to 100,527 in 1999.

Mother Tongue

Of the 1,103,695 residents tallied in the 2001 Census, 823,910 spoke only English, 44,335 spoke only French and 2675 spoke both French and English. Another 232,775 reported also speaking other languages.

The Name Game

When it comes to favourite choices for baby names, Manitobans' preferences are similar to much of the rest of the country. According to the Manitoba Vital Statistics Agency, Emily, Madison, Emma, Sarah and Hannah take the top five spots when it comes to favourite girl's names matching nation-wide preferences. Manitobans and other Canadians agree on the boy's names Ethan, Matthew and Joshua within the top five; Noah and Logan are in the ranks in Manitoba over Jacob and Nicolas in the rest of the country.

FROM NATIVE LANDS TO PROVINCIAL HANDS

Proudly Manitoban

Like many young folks I once looked across Manitoba thinking the grass was always greener in another province. Why, look at the mountains of BC, the rocky shores of Newfoundland and Labrador, the romantic and historic St. Lawrence. What I've since come to appreciate is what an eclectic and historically colourful place Manitoba really is. Diversity is the one constant in whatever corner of this province one chooses to explore. French and English settlers migrated here and immediately founded two new cultures among that of Canada's first peoples. Further immigration brought an influx of brave settlers from all corners of the world and with them unique perspectives and worldviews. Daring pioneers with challenging perspectives are what formed this prairie province and are what its foundation was built upon.

HOW MANITOBA CAME TO BE

First Footer

One of the first European explorers to have set foot in our fair province was Henry Hudson. He sailed into Hudson Bay in 1611.

A Few Years Later

The first official trading voyage into Manitoba began when the ship the *Nonsuch* landed on the shores of Hudson Bay in 1668. This led to the formation of the Hudson's Bay Company.

Trading Territory

The Hudson's Bay Company's fur trading rights mirrored the area covered by the Hudson's Bay watershed—from parts of Alberta to Ontario and south to Minnesota and North Dakota. The area was originally named Rupert's Land in honour of Prince Rupert's assistance in forming the company.

Putting Down Stakes

Manitoba's first settlement, the Red River Colony (also known as Selkirk Settlement) was founded by Lord Selkirk in 1812 where what is now downtown Winnipeg.

The Forks

The Red and Assiniboine rivers provided the province with its first, major transportation routes. The Assiniboine River flows into the Red River at what is now called "the Forks." By 1738, trading posts, such as Fort Rouge (erected by La Verendrye and considered the first French settlement in the area), were being established. Today, the 3.64 hectares overlooking the Red River to St. Boniface is a National Historic Site operated by Parks Canada.

Laying Track

By 1886, the Forks was emerging as the likely site for railway development. At one point the Northern Pacific and Manitoba Railway Company, the Canadian Northern, the Grand Trunk Pacific Railway and the Canadian National Railway claimed at least a piece of this site. Many of the buildings surviving in the area date back to this time.

Notable Events

Winnipeg was a booming city in the early 1900s, and much of its growth and success was a result of backbreaking labour by the working class. Feeling less than adequately repaid for their efforts, thoughts of taking action brewed, and the building and metal trade councils were formed. At the time, the only way for these new unions to gain recognition was for employers to be on board with the idea or for workers to walk off the job. For obvious reasons, employers weren't keen on the idea. Workers from these new councils banded together and appealed to the Trades and Labour Union in Winnipeg for a show of support. Together, workers from all parties—an amazing 30,000-plus workers in a city of 200,000—walked off the job on May 15, 1919. To say the city came to a standstill is an understatement. Even public employees, such as fire fighters, joined the action for a time. It wasn't until June 26 before the strike was called off. While for the most part the strike wasn't violent, a riot that came to be known as "Bloody Saturday" saw two people killed and about 30 injured.

DID YOU  KNOW?

Foreigners, particularly immigrants of eastern European descent, were blamed for Winnipeg's 1919 General Strike and called "bohunks" and "aliens" by local media. An article in the *New York Times* about the event was titled "Bolshevism Invades Canada." Interestingly, J.S. Woodsworth, one of the leaders of the strike, was a Methodist minister. He went on to found the country's first socialist party, the Co-operative Commonwealth Federation (CCF).

FOUNDING FATHERS

Misunderstood Maverick?

He was hailed as the "Father of Manitoba" and a hero to the Métis people, but a clear-cut understanding of the character of Louis Riel will likely never be without its controversy. Born in 1844, a young Louis studied theology (he was initially bound for the priesthood) and then law but ended both courses of study before he'd completed them. Still, he'd garnered a varied education for himself in the process and quickly put it to good use as an emerging Métis leader. When an expedition of surveyors led by the English-speaking governor William McDougall was looking to scout the Canadian government's newly acquired area of Rupert's Land with the goal of planning new settlements in the area, Riel and his people opposed the idea. Believing the Canadian government wasn't paying sufficient attention to the concerns of the Métis peoples, they reacted by establishing a provisional government. Such was the birth of the first Red River Rebellion. In the end, Riel's provisional government set the foundation for the province of Manitoba to enter Confederation in 1870.

During the course of this 1869–70 conflict, Riel ordered the execution of Thomas Scott, a soldier on the pro-Canadian side of the rebellion. This execution, which was thought an excessive penalty for Thomas' transgressions, resulted in British army officer Garnet Wolseley hunting Riel and Riel fleeing the country to Montana, but he didn't avoid a trial of his own altogether. In 1884, Reil returned to Canada and, ultimately, to the gallows' noose after being found guilty of high treason. To his death in 1885, though, Riel still thought himself a "divinely chosen leader and prophet."

Making Money for Farmers

"Be sure you are right, and then go ahead." With this phase as his personal motto and a sound business head on his shoulders, Nicholas Bawlf (1849–1914) took his prosperous flour, seed and grain business to a whole new level in the early 1880s. Bawlf believed that establishing a central marketplace for the buying and selling of these and other agricultural commodities would open up a world market for Manitoba farmers and make him and other merchants a decent living in the process. So in 1887, after an earlier failed attempt at the idea, he and 10 other merchants formed the Winnipeg Grain and Produce Exchange, now the Winnipeg Commodity Exchange, Inc. To say he made a living in the process is a bit of an understatement. In 1910, he was identified as "one of Winnipeg's famous 19 millionaires."

T-I-M-B-E-R!

Manitoba was once home to a thriving lumber industry, and one of the men at its helm was Theodore Arthur Burrows. Born in Ottawa in 1857, Burrows moved to Manitoba in 1875 and worked for a time surveying around the Dauphin area. Eventually he hit the books, earned a law degree from Manitoba College and became the first "articling student" in the province. Promising though his future may have seemed at that point, when approached by his uncle to join him in the family's real estate ventures Burrows jumped aboard. According to the Archives of Manitoba, the business was so successful that two North Winnipeg streets were named after the family—Alfred and Burrows. By 1878, Burrows took on yet another business venture with yet another uncle and the pair started up the Theodore A. Burrows Lumber Company the following year. Theodore's business adventures continued. That experience, coupled with his education, made him a prime candidate for public office, and from 1900 until 1908 he served as the Member of the Legislative Assembly for Dauphin. Although the lumber industry started to decline by the 1920s, at the height of his career as a lumber baron Theodore owned 15 sawmills and 35 lumber yards. In 1926, Theodore was appointed lieutenant-governor of Manitoba. He remained in that position until he died in 1929.

A Voice for Reform

Nellie McClung might have been born into a middle-class Ontario family in 1873, where she was likely taught to "know her place" as a woman in Canadian society, but she certainly wasn't of the temperament to pass her days as a quiet wallflower. Women's rights, the temperance movement, women's suffrage, health care, education—when it came to reform on these issues her voice was heard loud and clear.

Nellie moved with her family to homestead in Manitoba in 1880. An inquisitive youngster, much of her earlier education must have taken place in the family home since she wasn't able to attend school until the age of 10. Still, by 16 she'd become a certified teacher, and her first significant mark on the Manitoba public was by sharing her bright mind with her young students.

After her marriage to Robert Wesley McClung in 1896, Nellie refocused her attention on family and, as it happens, a career as a novelist. *Sowing Seeds in Danny*, published in 1908, was her first novel and a national bestseller.

By 1911, her family resettled in Winnipeg where she expanded her already abiding interest in the political scene. While successful at just about everything she put her mind to, it was in politics where she really made her mark. That "nice women did not want" the right to vote was an aberration. She and a group of her colleagues indirectly went toe-to-toe on the issue with then premier Rodmond Roblin, in a mock parliament. The satire depicted a parliament made up of women who were discussing the dangers and absurdities of allowing men the right to vote. The idiocy of it all was clearly exposed and, with help from

Nellie and her fellow suffragettes, Roblin's conservative government was defeated in the 1914 election. In 1916, the newly reining Liberal Party granted women the right to vote and run for public office, making Manitoba the first province in Canada to do so.

Soon after the 1914 election success, the McClungs moved to Alberta where Nellie continued her efforts at reform and equality. But it was in Manitoba where she first gained notoriety, and Manitoba proudly calls her one of its own.

Ballet Brilliance

Gweneth Lloyd was born in England in 1901 and moved to Winnipeg in 1938. Her love for dance was already well cultivated by the time she moved to Canada. She had graduated from a physical training program at Liverpool College and had completed a three-year course in Greek dancing in London. By the time she arrived in Winnipeg to live she'd also garnered extensive teaching experience, and together with a former student, Betty (Hey) Farrally, the pair opened the Canadian School of Ballet and the Winnipeg Ballet Club in 1939, renamed the Winnipeg Ballet in 1941. In 1951, the company gave a command performance for Their Royal Highnesses the Princess Elizabeth and the Duke of Edinburgh. In February 1953, the Royal Winnipeg Ballet was officially bestowed with the honour of becoming the first ballet company in the British Commonwealth to be granted a prestigious royal charter and thereafter was known as the Royal Winnipeg Ballet. Gweneth died in 1993.

POLITICS

Division of power

From 1870 to 1887 the chief ministers or provincial leaders of
Manitoba were not necessarily affiliated with any particular
political party. The provincial election of 1888 changed all that
when Thomas Greenway of the Liberal Party took the helm for
two years. A cursory glance at the premiers and their affiliate
party since then indicates that no election is a shoe-in. In the
15 governments to form since then, two were Conservative, two
were Liberal, one was United Farmers-Progressive, three were
Liberal-Progressive, four were Progressive Conservative (PC) and
three were New Democrat Party (NDP). While the Liberal or
Liberal Progressive parties reined for a time until 1958, since
then the government has been either PC or NDP.

Vote, Vote, Vote!

Thinking it a present-day problem, many an editorial has been
written scolding the public for not exercising the right to vote in
one election or another. But according to the Parliament of
Canada website, the problem is far from a recent one. The province with the poorest voter turnout in a federal election between
1867 and 2006 was Manitoba. Only 32 percent of eligible voters
cast a ballot on June 20, 1882.

Trouble at the Helm

The only Canadian Prime Minister to hail from Manitoba was
Arthur Meighen. The representative from Portage la Prairie
reigned from July 10, 1920, to December 28, 1921, but resigned
after he was defeated in his home riding in the general election
of December 6, 1921. He served as prime minister once again
from June 29 to September 24, 1926, but again resigned when
he was once again defeated in his home riding in the general
election of September 14, 1926.

Narrow Margins

John A. MacDonnell narrowly won the Selkirk riding on June 23, 1896. William F. McCreary repeated the feat, winning the riding on November 7, 1900, by a single vote.

Paving the Way
The first Native person to be elected federally was Errick French Willis, winning his Boissevain riding on July 28, 1930. The first Métis elected federally was Agnus Mckay. He won his Marquette riding in a by-election held March 2, 1871.

DID YOU KNOW?

First Nations people didn't have federal voting rights until 1960.

Aboriginal Leaders

After earlier failed attempts, Canada's First Nations once again sought to organize themselves politically in 1960, and by 1961, the National Indian Council was formed. Now known as the Assembly of First Nations, the first chief of the group was elected in 1968 and hailed from Saskatchewan. In fact, the Prairie Provinces have produced seven of the 11 chiefs, and four of them came from Manitoba: Ovide Mercredi served 1991–97, and Phil Fontaine served three terms—1997–2000, 2003–06 and 2006–present.

A Woman of Vision

Sharon Carstairs was born in Nova Scotia and entered politics in Alberta, but in Manitoba, she made her mark. She was the first woman to achieve several accomplishments: the first to lead a major political party (Liberal Party of Manitoba); to be elected Leader of the Official Opposition anywhere in Canada; to become Deputy Leader of the Government Senate of Canada (1997); and the first Manitoba woman to be named to a federal cabinet position (2001).

THE WEIGHT OF WAR

Remembered

I remember my mother telling me of her young years, growing up on the dusty prairie of small-town Saskatchewan. Some of those tales portray a vivid picture of the Great Depression. Others tell sad stories of young men going off to war, leaving sweethearts behind with little more than faint hope of their return—which many did not. The devastation of the battlefield showed itself perhaps most vividly in these rural communities across our fair country where 10 men losing their lives might have represented half the young male population. To name all the Manitobans who selflessly laid down their lives in the wars of the past century is simply not possible. What follows represents just a few of Manitoba's many war heroes but is, absolutely, a salute to them all.

Against All Odds

Leo Clarke (1892–1916)

Leo had barely enlisted in June 1915 before he lost his life on a battlefield of World War I. By September 1916, Leo was deep in hand-to-hand combat in the trenches near Pozieres, France. His entire battalion was wiped out on September 9—he alone remained standing. By the end of the day, he'd managed to kill 19 enemy soldiers and capture one. A month later, on October 11, Leo was again under enemy fire, this time in the Regina Trench, when an explosion displaced a large amount of earth, burying Leo and leaving him paralysed. He was taken to hospital but died eight days later. His father received Leo's Victoria Cross the following spring. It was presented by Edward William Spencer Cavandish, the 10th Duke of Devonshire, in front of a crowd of 30,000 people, representing the first time the Victoria Cross had been presented to a Commonwealth recipient in his own country.

I'll Do It

Robert Edward Cruickshank (1888–1961)

On May 1, 1918, Cruickshank, who was then a private, volunteered to take an important message from his platoon to his company headquarters. His efforts were thwarted time after time as he was repeatedly severely wounded, but he persisted and made a successful delivery and then was evacuated to a hospital in England. That October he received the Victoria Cross at Buckingham Palace with his mother and fiancée in attendance. One would think that would have been enough war for one lad, but when World War II was declared, Robert earned the rank of major with Canada's Home Guard.

The Ultimate Sacrifice

Frederick William Hall (1885–1915)

He was just 30 years old and already a company sergeant-major with the Winnipeg Rifles when he discovered men were missing from his platoon at the Second Battle of Ypres in Belgium. He could hear their moans and cries for help and knew them to be wounded. Twice, in the dark, he followed the sounds and returned with an injured soldier. In the early morning hours of April 24, 1915, Frederick noticed a wounded soldier not a dozen metres from his trench. Despite the fact they were being fired upon, Frederick made two attempts to reach the man and bring him to cover. During his second attempt, Frederick was shot through the head, dying instantly, and the wounded soldier was also killed.

DID YOU KNOW?

Winnipeg's Pine Street was renamed Valour Road in 1925. The move was an effort to recognize three war heroes—Leo Clarke, Frederick William Hall and Robert Shankland. All three men were Victoria Cross winners, and all three lived on the 700 block. It is thought to be the only street in the world to have been home to three Victoria Cross recipients.

True Friendship

Andrew Charles Mynarski (1916–44)

Saving a fellow officer was also how Andrew met with death.
A pilot with No. 419 "Moose" Squadron, Royal Canadian Air
Force, Andrew earned his air gunner wings just before Christmas
1941 and served in Halifax until going overseas in January 1942.
His last operation took place on June 12, 1944. The Avro
Lancaster he and his crew were serving on was attacked by an
enemy fighter over France. A fire broke out, and the captain in
charge ordered his crew to bail out. Andrew was on his way to
do so when he noticed his friend, Pat Brophy, pinned down by
the turret that mounted his gun. He tried to help his friend, but
to no avail, and by the time he finally gave in to the order to
jump, his pants and parachute had caught fire. His quick descent
added to the injuries caused by the fire, and Andrew died in hospital shortly after the incident. In a strange quirk of fate, Pat survived the crash and resulting explosion. Pat, along with his fellow
crewmembers who, on reuniting, heard of Andrew's gallant
efforts, successfully lobbied for Andrew to be awarded the
Victoria Cross and also to be posthumously recognized in the
rank of pilot officer.

Special Ops

Frank Herbert Dedrick Pickersgill (1915–44)

Frank was an unusual soldier in some ways. With two university
degrees, one in English and the other in classics, Frank had
plans to translate the great Jean-Paul Sartre's works into English.
But the war disrupted his plans, and although he was not the
kind of guy you could picture in the trenches, Frank had a lot
to offer. Along with his extensive education, he was multilin-
gual, speaking German, Latin, Greek, English and French flu-
ently. These skills landed him a job with the new Canadian
Intelligence Corps, where he worked closely with the British
Special Operations Executive. His efforts were short-lived, however. He and another Canadian, John Kenneth Macalister, were

assigned to the French Resistance, but shortly after descending by parachute into occupied France on June 20, 1943, the two men were captured and their French connections, who had been sent to meet them, were killed. Frank ended up in the Parisian Fresnes Prison, but it wasn't the first time he'd been in an enemy labour camp. He'd spent his first two years in a similar situation and escaped after someone gave him a hacksaw blade inserted into a loaf of bread. This time, though, luck was not on his side, and after a botched escape attempt, he was transported to Buchenwald concentration camp. On September 14, 1944, he was executed by the Nazis.

Attack and Counter-Attack

Robert Shankland (1887–1968)

As if combat isn't challenging enough, young Lieutenant Robert Shankland demonstrated perseverance, determination and calm, cool, collected thinking on October 26, 1917. Under his command, his platoon not only gained strategic position against their enemy at Passchendaele, Belgium, and continued to hold their ground, but they also attacked further, inflicting injuries on the enemy and pushing them to retreat. The lieutenant then managed to provide his commanding officers with valuable information that proved vital to the Commonwealth forces. Robert went on to the rank of lieutenant colonel and also served in World War II.

William, Sir William

Sir William Samuel Stephenson, CC, MC, DFC (1897–1989)

Known by the codename "Intrepid," Sir William represented the entire Western Hemisphere for British intelligence during World War II. Whether as a businessman, inventor, soldier or spy, Sir William earned the fearless title through the valiant way he attacked everything he did. By 19 years of age, he'd already been promoted to the rank of sergeant, and while recovering from being gassed, he learned to fly. He earned one accolade after another as a pilot with the British Royal Flying Corps, climbing to the rank of captain by the end of World War I and receiving the Distinguished Flying Cross and the Military Cross along the way. At this point he was only 21 years old, but his heroic efforts didn't end there. Although he was born in Winnipeg, at this point he'd made a life for himself in Britain. By 1936, his career as an international spy had taken hold, and he was providing the British government with Nazi military secrets. His work in secret intelligence continued throughout World War II when he headed up the British Security Coordination (BSC) in New York City. His responsibilities included gathering enemy intelligence, providing security to protect the British against sabotage and to "organize American public opinion in favour of aid to Britain." Amazingly enough, Sir William (an affluent man by this point, thanks to his between-war business activities) didn't take a penny for his efforts and paid his cohorts out of his own pocket. He is also credited with establishing Whitby, Ontario's Camp X—a wartime training ground for British, Canadian and American "covert operators." While he was knighted by the British government for his efforts in 1945 and received the Presidential Medal for Merit from the U.S. government in 1946, it wasn't until 1979 that he was recognized by Canada. On December 17 of that year, Stephanson was made a Companion of the Order of Canada. It is widely believed Intrepid was the inspiration for the character of James Bond.

In the Trenches

In 1916, combat trenches were dug around Winnipeg's Main Street and Water Avenue. They were used as part of a recruiting and training drive for World War I.

DID YOU KNOW?

Manitoba declared 2006 the Year of the War Bride.

BUSY BEAVERS

Diversification

Manitoba might not have the big money lure of black gold to offer, but the province boasts opportunities in a wide area of industry. From the traditional family farm to mining and smelting, science, technology, manufacturing, finance and tourism. Manitoba prides itself on having one of the most diversified economies in the country.

Industry	Percentage of GDP
Finance, Insurance & Real Estate	20
Manufacturing	13
Trade	13
Transportation & Warehousing	7
Government	7
Construction	5
Information, Culture, Arts & Entertainment	5
Agriculture	4
Utilities	3
Mining & Other Primary	2
Other Services	21

The Garment District

Winnipeg was once home to a huge garment industry. About 8000 workers were employed in 1986, and while that number has decreased it's estimated 5000 Winnipeggers, mostly women, still make their living this way.

TRANSPORTATION

By the Numbers

Manitoba has 51 provincial highways and roughly 237 provincial roads. Main route highways are numbered from 1 to 99, with "loop route" numbers beginning at 100. Secondary highways or provincial roads are numbered from 200 to 599.

Just Passing Through

Whether it's by train, plane, truck or ship, Manitoba's transportation and warehousing industry pumps a heavy $2.2 billion into the province's gross domestic product. Of that, $1.18 billion comes through the trucking industry.

Riding the Rails

Together the Canadian National (CN) and Canadian Pacific Railway (CPR) maintain about 2439 kilometres of rail lines in Manitoba. The CPR was the first company to lay track in the province.

The Competition

Another 1775 kilometres of track is maintained by five regional or short-line railway companies: the Hudson Bay Railway, Southern Manitoba Railway, Burlington Northern Santa Fe Manitoba, Greater Winnipeg Water District Railway and Central Manitoba Railway.

DID YOU KNOW?

The Red River cart is a common symbol of Métis nationalism.

Flying High

Winnipeg's James Armstrong Richardson International Airport is the country's eighth busiest airport. It's also one of only a few 24-hour, unrestricted airports in the nation. Originally known as the Winnipeg International Airport, it was renamed on December 10, 2006, in a formal ceremony to pay tribute to James Armstrong Richardson, Sr. A Canadian aviation pioneer who lived most of his years in Winnipeg, Richardson Sr. is credited with founding Western Canadian Airways in 1926. The company evolved into Canadian Airways and was later incorporated into Trans-Canada Air Lines, the precursor to Air Canada.

Farther than the Eye Can See

Highway 75 begins in Winnipeg and travels directly south for a long, long way. In fact, the highway continues into the United States, turning into Interstate 29, and on that you can motor on all the way down to Mexico.

Conquering the Red

Steamboats first started appearing on the Red River around 1859. Until the advent of railway travel, steamers such as the *Selkirk* were the most effective way of transporting passengers, supplies and food staples to various Manitoba settlements.

Site Specific

While travel by wooden carts and covered wagons wasn't unusual for settlers in the Americas, pioneers travelling along the Red River, from St. Paul, Minnesota, and Pembina, North Dakota, to Winnipeg (then Fort Garry) and north to Edmonton (Upper Fort des Prairies) used a vehicle unique to the area. The two-wheel Red River cart, made from oak and secured together with animal sinew, was usually ox-driven. Folks used it to transport supplies north and furs back south. Oxen were strong enough to pull heavy loads and, according to the Manitoba Historical Society, though they travelled only a few kilometres an hour, they could typically cover between 30 and 40 kilometres per day. The two-wheeled wonder was invented by the Métis people and used from the mid-19th century until the turn of the 20th century.

Manufacturing Milestone

Motor Coach Industries might be an international company currently headquartered in Illinois, but it had its humble beginnings in Winnipeg. When it was originally founded and incorporated by Harry Zoltok in 1932, it was named Fort Garry Motor Body and Paint Works Limited, and its specialty was building buses. Greyhound Lines of Canada, then a major customer, bought shares in the company in 1948 and purchased it completely in 1958. The company maintains a manufacturing plant in Winnipeg along with another in Pembina, North Dakota.

NATURAL RESOURCES

Mining for Metals

Mining in Manitoba accounts for more than $1 billion in production each year, making it the second largest primary resource industry in the province. There are currently eight operating mines in the province. Most are located in the northern portions of the province near the communities of Thompson, Flin Flon, Snow Lake and Bissett. The Tanco Mine, located near Lac du Bonnet, is the only exception.

Salty Tales
The first commercially developed mineral in the province was salt. Brine springs located in parts of Lake Manitoba and Lake Winnipegosis were discovered in the early 1800s and were mined commercially until 1978.

Value in Stone
Pockets of stone valued for construction have been mined in areas of Manitoba since settlers first came to the province, and many communities bear witness to the fact in their names. Sand, gravel and crushed stone are mined just south of Stonewall, and

a quarry of limestone (also known as Tyndall stone) has been in operation near Tyndall since 1895. A gypsum plant was also opened in the Interlake region in 1901.

All That Glitters
The discovery of gold in Manitoba first occurred at Rice Lake in 1911. Gold was first mined at the Central Manitoba Mine near Bissett from 1933 to 1968, and then again from 1990 to 2000. Other gold deposits have been found near Snow Lake in 1925.

Black Gold
Manitoba might not produce as much oil as Alberta, but it is considered to be of relatively high quality. It was 1951 when crude oil was first discovered in the province. In 2001 alone, 104 new wells measuring 34,020 metres collectively were drilled.

Copper and Zinc
The 1922 discovery of copper and zinc at Cold Lake led to the subsequent establishment of the Sherridon Mine. The Hudson Bay Mining & Smelting Co. has also been mining in the nearby Flin Flon area for more than 70 years. As recently as 1993, large copper and zinc deposits were discovered directly beneath the city of Flin Flon—large enough, in fact, to keep the company busy until 2016 at that site alone.

Rare Find
Tantalum is a rare metallic element often used in the making of dental and surgical instruments. In 1969, tantalum was discovered at Bernic Lake and shortly thereafter the first and only tantalum mine on the continent was opened near Lac du Bonnet.

DID YOU KNOW?

Since 1939, peat moss has been harvested in the southeastern portions of the province for the horticultural and agricultural industries.

The Power of Water

Owners of the Grant Mill were the first to try their hand at harnessing the power of water to make electricity back in 1829. It was not successful. It wasn't until March 12, 1873, when the Manitoba Electric and Gas Light Company successfully provided the public with power. It demonstrated its success by flooding the Davis House Hotel with light. Here are a few more hydroelectric tidbits:

- The first hydroelectric plant was located north of Brandon and ran from 1900 to 1924

- The first attempt to harness the power of the Winnipeg River occurred near Pinawa in 1906

- Power was provided to some communities outside of Winnipeg in 1916

- By 1955, Manitoba had three utility providers: the Manitoba Power Commission and Manitoba Hydro Electric Board were both operated by the provincial government, while the capital city ran the Winnipeg Hydro Electric System

- In 1961, the two provincial power providers merged to form Manitoba Hydro

- In 1999, Centra Gas Manitoba was bought out by Manitoba Hydro

AGRICULTURE

Farm Front

Agriculture brings $3.9 billion into Manitoba's economy. Hogs, canola, wheat, cattle, dairy products, oats, poultry, eggs, flaxseed and barley are the largest contributors to the agriculture sector.

Potatoes Anyone?

Carberry's economy is intrinsically tied to potatoes. Back in 1959, when grains grew in abundance and quotas were low, farmers in the Carberry area decided they needed to diversify a little and after consulting with provincial specialists on the matter, they thought that growing potatoes seemed like a good idea. But it wasn't until 1960, after the old airport was purchased and refurbished into a processing plant, that the first 120 hectares were planted. Today, the processing plant, which since October 2004 has been owned by McCain Foods Canada, employs 500 people to process the 7285 hectares of potatoes grown in the North Cypress area surrounding Carberry. From this point of origin, millions of tonnes of potato products are shipped around the world each year. (And in case you weren't aware, when you enter the town of Carberry, you'll likely notice the town sign that says, "Carberry Welcomes you to King Spud Country.")

The Port of Grain

Churchill's largest shipping responsibility is in grain. It accounts for about 90 percent of the port's traffic and in 2004 shipped more than 384,000 tonnes of the product.

Fungus-free Food

Bread is a nutritional staple in most diets around the world, so when a rust-type fungus hit prairie wheat crops in 1916, it not only hurt farmers' pocketbooks, it threatened the food supply. Within a year, Margaret Newton—a researcher with Winnipeg's Dominion Rust Research Centre—developed several varieties of rust-resistant wheat, making life less worrisome for Manitoba farmers. The year was 1917—four years before she made history again as the first woman in Canada to earn a Ph.D. in agriculture science.

INVENTIONS

Environmental Consciousness

Winnipeg's Dr. Elaine Thompson, disturbed by the excess waste left by discarded, old tires, set to work on inventing a way to reuse them. Her idea was to find a way to remove the rubber, remake it into an asphalt emulsion and use the end product to resurface damaged roads. Her invention was patented in 1982.

Nuclear Research

The formation of the Atomic Bomb has a Winnipeg connection. Born in the city's North End in 1910, Louis Slotin was raised and educated in Winnipeg and earned several academic honours along the way. Yet, all was not easy for the award-winning academic. In 1937, he'd been turned down for a position with the National

Research Council of Canada and ended up as a research associate at the University of Chicago instead. After two years of long hours, tedious work and almost no pay, his efforts were finally recognized and he took a position with Chicago's Metallurgical Laboratory of the Manhattan Project. His contribution to the atomic bomb was in the development of its triggering device. He died on May 21, 1946, after using his body to stop the escape of radiation from a plutonium bomb core he and seven of his colleagues were working on. His colleagues survived, but Slotin died nine days later. His story formed the basis of several books and films, including the 1999 Hollywood movie *Fat Man and Little Boy*.

Animation Inspiration

While it's admittedly a stretch to call this one a Winnipeg invention, the story behind the "bear of very little brain" was most definitely a Winnipeg innovation. The story began when Lieutenant Harry Colebourn met a hunter and a bear cub at a train station in River Bend Ontario. The hunter was on his way home to fatten the youngster before making bear stew out of him. Colebourn, a veterinarian, was of course appalled and immediately sought about getting the cub away from the hunter by plying him with a $20 bill. Colebourn, an officer with the 34th Fort Garry Horse of Manitoba, thought he could take the bear with him to his next posting with the Canadian Army Veterinary Corps in Valcartier, Québec, reasoning it would make a great mascot for the 2nd Canadian Infantry Brigade.

Colebourn ended up transporting the bear, whom he'd named Winnie after his home town of Winnipeg, to London, England. He planned to leave the bear at the zoo for a short time, but when he didn't return for four years, Colebourn realized the bear had made a home for herself there and it would be wrong to move her.

Enter A.A. Milne. The British author and his young son were taken by the bear, and voila, a children's classic was born with the creation of *Winnie the Pooh*.

To commemorate old Winnie, the members of the 34th Fort Garry Horse erected a bronze statue of Winnie and his rescuer in 1999, first at the London Zoo and then in Winnipeg.

New and Improved

While baby snugglies have been around for a while, Winnipeg mom Judy Pettersen just couldn't find one that was comfortable. With a fussy baby and a house full of chores staring at her, the uncomfortable snuggly was definitely a problem. As the old adage goes, necessity is the mother of invention. The tired mom set out to accomplish yet one more chore—inventing a baby backpack that was both functional and comfortable. By the time she had her third youngster, her idea had transformed into a reality, and the BabyTrekker was born. Before long what began as an idea to make her own life a little easier had grown into a cottage industry that required its own manufacturing plant, and in 1997, her efforts garnered her the Manitoba Home Business Woman of the Year award.

COST OF LIVING

Lucky to Live Here

Living in a First World country makes it all too easy to become complacent and forget there are people who are homeless and that some folks might have a hard time coughing up the money they need for prescription medication. Overall, Manitoba has a high standard of living.

A Roof Over Your Head

While housing costs in cities such as Edmonton, Vancouver and Toronto continue to skyrocket, a family home is still relatively affordable in Winnipeg. The October 2006 Canadian Real Estate Association forecast reported an average family home in Canada cost approximately $277,700. That was expected to rise to $294,400 in 2007. Of the country's 10 provinces, it costs more to put a roof over your head in British Columbia than anywhere else, with an average cost in 2007 expected in the $421,800 range. Alberta isn't far behind with houses there averaging at the $305,100 mark. So for folks wanting a nice home in a more reasonable price range, Manitoba fits the bill quite nicely. The average projected price for a family home in 2007 is expected to be in the $164,300 range. Not bad, eh?

Affordable and Friendly

Step aside Alberta, Manitoba's advantage is a superior quality of living with lower personal costs and taxes. For example, Manitoba ranks second-lowest combined taxes and living costs in the country for a single person with an annual income of $30,000 per year and for a double income family of four earning $60,000 per year. First place in these categories is Saskatchewan, where if yours is a family of four with only one annual income, your taxes and living costs are the lowest in the country.

Jobs, Jobs, Jobs

Statistics maintained by the Manitoba Bureau of Statistics indicate the province's unemployment rate from 2000 to 2005 was consistently lower than the national average.

	2000	2001	2002	2003	2004	2005
Canada	6.9%	7%	8%	8%	7%	6.8%
Manitoba	5%	5%	5%	5%	5%	4.8%

HEALTH

Life Expectancy

Canadians are generally a healthy lot. An average Canadian man can expect to live to a ripe old age of 77.8 years, but that's still significantly less than their female counterparts. Canadian women, on average, can expect to live to 82.6 years. Still, these figures fluctuate somewhat across the country with Manitoba falling somewhere in the middle. Here are some 2004 comparisons from Statistics Canada, released in December 2006.

Province	Men (years)	Women (years)
Newfoundland/Labrador	75.8	81.3
Prince Edward Island	76.8	81.6
Nova Scotia	76.5	81.6
New Brunswick	77.0	82.2
Quebec	77.5	82.6
Ontario	78.3	82.7
Manitoba	**76.4**	**81.4**
Saskatchewan	76.6	82.1
Alberta	77.8	82.6
British Columbia	78.7	83.1
Yukon	74.5	78.6
Northwest Territories	78.4	81.7
Nunavut	66.8	74.2

On the Rise

Since 1978, Manitobans, along with most Canadians, have witnessed their life expectancy rise by between three and four years.

Sad Statistics

According to Statistics Canada, one way to measure the health status of a nation is by looking at its infant mortality rates. Based on 2003 statistics, Canada's infant mortality rate is 5.0 per 1000 live births for boys and 3.8 per 1000 live births for girls. Sadly, Manitoba's statistics are considerably more dismal, with the infant mortality rate measuring 8.5 per 1000 live births for boys and 4.6 per 1000 live births for girls.

Obesity in Youth

According to some sources, Manitoba's young people aren't in the greatest shape. In the last 25 years, more than twice the number of youngsters aged 12 to 17 are overweight and the obesity rate has tripled. Here are a few more troubling statistics:

- ☛ 31 percent of Manitoba youth aged 12 to 17 are overweight or obese, compared with the national statistic of 26 percent
- ☛ 59 percent of Manitoba youth aged 12 to 19 need to increase their activity to remain healthy
- ☛ Manitoba's children aged 2 to 11 spend an estimated 14.5 hours watching television each week
- ☛ Manitoba teens aren't far behind, spending an estimated 12.5 hours a week in front of the television

Heartfelt Discovery

Manitoba made medical history in 1950 after Dr. John Alexander "Jack" Hopps revealed the first prototype of his mechanical heart. The electrical engineer stumbled across the idea for what would come to be known as the pacemaker while conducting experiments on hypothermia with fellow researchers Dr. Wilfred Bigelow and

Dr. John Callaghan in 1949. Bigelow had noticed a heart that had stopped beating started up again after probing the left ventricle. Hopps decided to delve into the history books to see if anyone else had experimented with reviving the heart and came across the work of Dr. Sweet and physiologists Carl Wiggers and William Kouwenhoven. Though it wasn't much, it was enough to encourage Hopps to continue with an idea he had. What he envisioned was a pacemaker that "would fire steady, metered, electrical impulses to control a patient's heart rate." His 1950 model was far too large to implant into a human chest. It took him another eight years of refining his prototype before a useable pacemaker was created.

DID YOU  KNOW?

Dr. John Alexander "Jack" Hopps, inventor of the pacemaker, benefited from his own invention when he was the recipient of a pacemaker to correct an erratic heartbeat. In 1999, just a year after he died, Hopps' invention was recognized as the top Canadian engineering achievement in the 20th century.

Leading the Nation

The Canadian Science Centre for Human and Animal Health in Winnipeg is a research facility focused on the study of both human and animal disease. The centre is the first in the world to accommodate both human and animal health facilities at the highest level of biocontainment under one roof. The centre is also the first in the country to house a Level Four lab—the National Microbiology Laboratory studies treatment and vaccine possibilities for otherwise fatal diseases such as the Ebola virus. Here's how the centre keeps everyone safe from the deadly bacteria being studied:

- ☞ laboratories in the Level Three and Four categories are equipped with completely airtight rooms;

- ☞ the centre's special air filtration system traps particles 85 times smaller than the smallest known disease-causing agent;

- ☞ all solid and liquid wastes are sterilized.

 DID YOU KNOW?

The only labs in the world where you'll find samples of the deadly 1918 Spanish flu virus are at Winnipeg's National Microbiology Laboratory and the Centre for Disease Control in the U.S.

Ebola Breakthrough

In January 2007, Winnipeg's National Microbiology Laboratory released news that researchers had developed an Ebola vaccine that was successful in four of eight trials. This was the first time a vaccine had been successful in fighting off the virus in a previously exposed subject. There is a 90 percent mortality in people exposed to the strain of Ebola virus studied in their experiment.

A Personal Journey

Winnipeger David Reimer's very personal story begins in 1966 at the age of six months when it was discovered he (then named Bruce) and his twin brother Brian had trouble urinating because of tight foreskin. Doctors decided to perform a circumcision two months later. Bruce went first, but the surgery didn't go well. His penis was destroyed. Of course, his brother's procedure was cancelled, but that didn't help Bruce.

His parents, obviously distressed, opted to take their son to Johns Hopkins Medical Centre in Baltimore, Maryland. Their goal was to visit then renowned psychologist John Money. His specialty was sexual development and, in particular, gender identity. He argued that sexual identity was something that was learned, not innate, and that Bruce could just as easily learn to be a girl as a boy. Since replacing a penis at that time was considered impossible, and surgically constructing a vagina well within the realm of possibility, at the age of 22 months, Bruce was transformed into Brenda.

David's story tells of how years of ongoing therapy with Money, contrary to the doctor's reports, didn't help him feel like a girl. At school, Brenda was teased and bullied, and it didn't matter what anyone did, Brenda didn't feel at all like a girl. At the age of 15, she threatened suicide if her parents made her take another session with Money.

David went public with his story in 1997 in the hope that no one else would ever travel the painful course he had. By then he had gone through another gender reassignment and was again a man. He was married and had three stepchildren. Sadly, going public put too much strain on his marriage, and it ended in divorce. His brother, Brian, didn't come through unscathed. In 2002 he died of a "toxic combination of alcohol and antidepressants." David committed suicide in 2004.

Although he was a writer, David's story was written by John Colapinto under the title *As Nature Made Him: The Boy Who Was raised as a Girl* and published by HarperCollins in 2000. In 2005, the story was used as the basis for an episode of *Law & Order: Special Victims Unit* called "Identity."

The Iron Rose

The small, rural community of Whitemouth might not have a lot to offer by way of modern conveniences. It doesn't have an all-night diner, a super mall or a big box Wal-Mart. It is a community rich in heritage; if you ask any long-standing resident if they can name a significant figure in their community's history, chances are many would speak of Dr. Charlotte Ross. Lovingly called the Iron Rose, Dr. Ross was Manitoba's first practicing female physician. That's just the beginning of her amazing story.

Dr. Ross braved what was in 1881 little more than a wild countryside, accompanying her husband David, who had taken up employment in Whitemouth's then-thriving lumber industry. With a deep, abiding calling to become a doctor, she'd been forced to study medicine at the Women's Medical College of Pennsylvania, since no Canadian schools of the day would admit women to what was considered strictly a man's field of study. On her arrival in Whitemouth, she naively thought she'd be caring for the women and children of the area. She had no clue that simply by arriving and settling there she'd be making history as the first white woman in the area. And before she knew it, her skills as a physician were called upon, in one circumstance or another, from treating life-threatening injuries to nursing folks through serious illnesses.

The only doctor from Whitemouth to Winnipeg, more than 100 kilometres away, she rapidly gained the respect of area residents. But the powers that be were another matter. As a woman in a male-dominated profession, Dr. Ross was considered little more than a charlatan. Several times she was threatened with prosecution by the Manitoba College of Physicians and Surgeons and, ultimately, imprisonment if she didn't stop practicing. When women were finally accepted in Canadian medical schools, Dr. Ross was told she must to go back to school if she wanted to practise medicine. She flatly refused. She had paid her dues once, and she wasn't about to succumb to pressure to unnecessarily recertify, even from the Manitoba government.

Dr. Ross practised medicine in the area for 25 years before retiring at the age of 69 years in 1912. She died four years later. It wasn't until 1993 when her contribution to the settlement of Manitoba was recognized by the province she so tirelessly served.

A Special Heart

Beatrice Cyr St. Amant (1888–1957) was a teacher by training, but her love for children went beyond just their education. Widowed when her son Gerard was just 10 months old, Beatrice returned to the classroom, but only for a short while. By the time Gerard was five, he was experiencing debilitating epileptic seizures and eventually had to withdraw from school. By 1939 his mother decided to quit her job to care for him full time since she was unable to get appropriate care for him. Realizing nothing was available for families of children with special needs, Beatrice founded St. Amant (then the Youville Epileptic Hospital). So until 1956 she cared for her son and other children with epilepsy or other mental or physical challenges. After the *Winnipeg Tribune* published reports on her work in 1954, her efforts attracted attention across the continent, and folks were referring to her as "a kind of Florence Nightingale." Today, St. Amant is part of the Catholic Health Network.

EDUCATION

Literacy

It's easy to forget that there are a lot of people who, for whatever reason, can't read well enough to cope in today's society. In 1991, Statistics Canada stated that less than 50 percent of Canada's workforce could read at a college level, and by 2000 that level of literacy would be required by 70 percent of the workforce. What follows are a few more facts and figures that will likely leave you scratching your head in wonder:

- ☞ As many as 180,000 Manitoban adults are considered "illiterate or functionally illiterate"
- ☞ About 39,000 Manitoban adults aged 20 to 64 have less than a grade nine education
- ☞ More than one in four (or about 180,380) Manitoban adults aged 20 to 64 did not receive their high school diploma
- ☞ About 22.5 percent of adults aged 20 to 34 did not receive their high school diploma
- ☞ About 25.6 percent of adults aged 35 to 44 did not receive their high school diploma
- ☞ About 34.3 percent of adults aged 45 to 64 did not receive their high school diploma
- ☞ Statistics for Manitoba's Native peoples are even more dismal with 40 to 70 percent of the adult population aged 20 to 64 (depending on the community) having less than a grade nine education
- ☞ If you live in Manitoba and have a college or trade school certificate, you could expect an average annual salary of about $29,000
- ☞ If you live in Manitoba and don't have a high school diploma you can expect an average annual salary of about $19,000

The Language Debate

Manitoba's original Constitution of 1870 guaranteed students of French families a provincially funded, separate school system—in fact, it guaranteed English- and French-speaking Manitobans equal rights. By 1890, the Manitoba Schools Act changed those initial intentions. It effectively abolished French as a second official language and cut all provincial funding to Catholic (which were French-run) schools.

A compromise on what quickly became known as the Manitoba Schools Question was reached by Sir Wilfred Laurier's government of 1896. Laurier and Manitoba's premier of the day, Thomas Greenway, agreed that a Catholic education would still be provided in public schools, and for schools with at least 10 French-speaking students, French could also be used in teaching. A Catholic school board was also re-established but without government funding. The end result didn't really satisfy Manitoba's considerable French-speaking population, and when even an appeal to Pope Leo XIII didn't change the situation, many French Canadians left the province. By 1916, all French instruction was removed from classrooms, and English was the only official language. But the French–English debate didn't end there. Although according to the Canadian Constitution Act of 1982, the only officially bilingual province in the country is New Brunswick, Manitoba prides itself on its French heritage and boasts everything from bilingual street signs to being a heavy proponent of French immersion.

French Immersion

Manitoba's efforts at encouraging youth to become bilingual have a long history. The first French immersion program in the province was established at Ecole Sacre-Coeur in 1973. In 1976, the Bureau de l'Education Francaise was directed by the Manitoba Department of Education to further develop and maintain French as a first language and French immersion programs. Then, in 1995, Manitoba's French immersion program passed a major milestone when it was recognized by the province's Department of Education as one of its four official programs alongside the English program, French program and the senior years technology education program.

Multilingual Opportunities

Aside from promoting the French language, the Department of Education supports several other languages in provincial schools for up to 50 percent of instruction in their bilingual heritage language programming, including Cree, Filipino, German, Hebrew, Japanese, Mandarin, Ojibwe, Portuguese, Spanish and Ukrainian.

- About 1587 students in kindergarten to grade six are in bilingual programs
- About 250 students in grade seven to senior four (grade 12) are enrolled in "enhanced" language programs
- Of these language options, German has the highest province-wide enrolment, according to 2004–05 school year statistics, followed by Spanish
- In Winnipeg, Spanish ranks most popular, followed by Filipino, Japanese, Ojibwe and Cree
- Manitoba schools first offered Japanese as an option in 1994

Back in the Day

Before Manitoba began consolidating provincial schools into districts in the 1950s, there were more than 1000 one-room schoolhouses.

Ohr Ha Torah

Winnipeg is home to one Orthodox Jewish school. The Ohr Ha Torah Day School was founded in 1998 by a group of parents wanting to provide their youngsters with a concentrated religious studies program. Included with the secular curriculum requirements is a focus on Judaic studies, adherence to the Torah and observance of Mitzvot.

Cindy Klassen, five-time Olympic medallist in speed skating at the 2006 Winter Olympics, is a graduate of Winnipeg's Mennonite Brethren Collegiate Institute. The school, founded in 1945, has about 550 students enrolled in grades 6 to 12 each year.

Tried and True

Founded by the Grey Nuns in 1869, Winnipeg's St. Mary's Academy is the "oldest continuously operating independent school in the province." The all-girl, private Catholic school enrols about 550 students each year.

More than Just Sports

Founded in 1926 by the Oblate fathers, St. Paul's High School has earned itself a stellar reputation when it comes to sports. In 2006, it was the AAA Football Champions Varsity, won Junior Varsity and Freshmen Volleyball Provincial Championships, as well as the Junior Varsity boys cross-country provincial championship. The school also shines when it comes to producing alumni gifted in other walks of life. Among these notable graduates are former federal cabinet minister Reggie Alcock, Microsoft programmer and creator of the computer game Minesweeper Robert Donner and Manitoba premier Gary Doer.

Continuing Education

Manitoba is home to at least 18 post-secondary institutions ranging in focus from theological studies to business, trade and academic vocations.

- The University of Manitoba was founded in 1877 and is the province's largest university. It takes 2348 staff members to fine tune the 24,267 undergraduates and 3332 postgraduates studying there.
- Manitoba College (1871) and Wesley College (1888) together formed United College in 1938. In 1967, a new charter was formed, and the institution was renamed the University of Winnipeg. In 2004, the university was likely one of few not put off by regular magazine polls after Maclean's Magazine released the results of its University Graduate Survey. The findings put the University of Winnipeg in the "Top Ten of All Canadian Universities."
- The College Universitaire de Saint-Boniface started off as an all-boys school in 1818. Although it is located in the heart of St. Boniface, the college is affiliated with the University of Manitoba.
- The Canadian Mennonite University's Outtatown program provides students with six months of travel studies that take them throughout western Canada and then to Guatemala or South Africa.
- Red River College is based in Winnipeg but offers courses in satellite classrooms in smaller communities throughout the province, including Gimli, Steinbach, Portage la Prairie and Winkler.
- Brandon University was founded as a Baptist institution in 1900. Then known as Brandon College, it wasn't a chartered university until 1967.
- Other post-secondary schools are CDI College, Herzing College, Assiniboine Community College, Keewatin Community College, Providence College and Seminary, Steinbach Bible College, St. Andrew's College, St. John's College, St., Paul's College, William and Catherine Booth College, Winnipeg Technical College and Canadian Nazarene College.

LITERATURE

"Too Prairie"

I remember asking a small Ontario bookseller once why she didn't carry more books by Manitoba authors. "They're too prairie," she simply said. I didn't quite get what she meant until I moved to northern British Columbia and started to read BC authors. I noticed the regional quality to their work right away, and before long I missed my prairie-grown literature. I could appreciate these BC authors, as well as British, American and (since I'm sadly unilingual) any author who writes in English for that matter. Yet, there is something I find so rich and vibrant and alive about Manitoba authors. It's clear to see our country's literature is greatly influenced by the voices of Manitoba writers who have helped garner Canadian wordsmiths everywhere the attention they deserve. Indeed, Manitoban artists of many genres and art forms are to be celebrated for their valuable contribution to Canadian and international art, music, theatre, cinema and dance as well.

David Arnason (1940–)

One news report quotes David saying, "If you wait until you feel like writing, you will never write." Arnason's disciplined, 1000-word-a-day target has helped propel him through publishing 13 books—and there doesn't appear to be an end in sight for this prolific author.

David Bergen (1957–)

A relative newcomer on the scene, David's first novel, *A Year of the Lesser* (1996), earned a Notable Book mention by the *New York Times*. So far he's published four novels and one short story collection.

Margaret Laurence (1926–87)

Margaret was born in Neepawa and, despite losing both her parents at a young age, considered herself "an extremely fortunate child." Her early interests in reading and writing were consistently encouraged by all family members, and she was writing articles for the *Neepawa Press* by grade 11. During her prolific career she published 17 books, her first in 1961 called *This Side Jordan*. Five of her novels, considered the Manawaka series, were based on the community of Neepawa. Margaret died in January 1987, and her ashes were laid to rest at Neepawa's Riverside Cemetery on June 23. The next day marked the opening of the Margaret Laurence Home, a museum created in her honour in the home where she lived as a youngster. Her work earned her two Governor General's Awards, one in 1967 and another in 1975.

Marshall McLuhan (1911–80)

Well known for coining the phrases "the medium is the message" and "global village," Marshall was a brilliant communicator, philosopher and educator and is often considered the most celebrated teacher of the 20th century.

Martha Ostenso (1900–63)

A romance between Martha, then a student at the University of Manitoba, and a professor of English named Douglas Durkin eventually drew this literary star from our fair province. Still, her most famous work, *Wild Geese*, was set in the province's Interlake region and was her only novel set in Canada. It earned her a $13,500 first prize in a nationwide American competition (she was up against 1700 entries) and was eventually made into a silent movie and later remade for Hollywood, titled *After the Harvest* (2001). Henry Fonda took the leading role.

Gabrielle Roy (1909–83)
Born in St. Boniface, Gabrielle gained notoriety almost as soon as her first novel, *Bonheur d'Occasion* (1945) was released. Its depiction of a working-class Montreal neighbourhood is commonly considered as an impetus in Québec's Quiet Revolution of the 1960s. Two years later the book was published as *The Tin Flute* in English, earned the 1947 Governor General's Award and sold more than three-quarters of a million copies in the U.S.

Carol Shields (1935–2003)
Although she was born in Oak Park, Illinois, Winnipeg lays claim to this brilliant literary voice because of the 20 years, 1980–2000, when she lived in the city. She held various positions from professor at the University of Manitoba to chancellor at the University of Winnipeg. During her career, Shields wrote 10 novels, four short story collections, three books of poetry, six plays, one book of criticism and one biography and edited two anthologies, making her prolific in almost every genre. Among her many accolades, she was awarded the Governor General's Award for her novel *The Stone Diaries* in 1993. Two years later that same novel was awarded the Pulitzer Prize for fiction, giving it the distinction of being the only book to win both awards.

Miriam Toews (1964–)
A novelist and humorist of Mennonite stock, Miriam's breakthrough novel *A Complicated Kindness* (2004) raised a few eyebrows in the province's bible belt. Nevertheless, the story of a 16-year-old girl looking to escape her Russian Mennonite roots in exchange for the slums of New York City sat on the Canadian bestseller list for a year and earned Miriam a Governor General's Award for Fiction and a Giller Prize nomination.

A.E. van Vogt (1912–2000)

A.E. began his career writing for pulp magazines such as *True Story*, but by the end of his career he'd earned the recognition of science-fiction lovers everywhere. The 1940s was considered by some as the "Golden Age of Science Fiction" and was a time when A.E. really shone. Some compare his influence to the great Isaac Asimov.

Adele Wiseman (1928–92)

As a daughter of Russian-Jewish parents, both of Adele's novels deal with Jewish immigration and the challenges of adapting to Canadian society. Her first novel, *The Sacrifice*, was published in 1956 and earned her the Governor General's Award for Fiction.

George Woodcock (1912–95)

A poet and non-fiction writer, George is likely best known for founding *Canadian Literature* in 1959, the first journal dedicated to Canadian writing. Among his numerous accolades is the Governor General's Award for his critical work *The Crystal Spirit* (1966). He was asked to accept the Order of Canada but refused because it wasn't an award bestowed on him by his peers.

Making a Difference

Dorothy Livesay (1909–1996)

There's something about the Manitoba air that produces free-thinkers, folks who aren't afraid to challenge the status quo, and poet Dorothy Livesay is certainly proof of that sentiment. Born on a snowy day in October 1909, Dorothy grew into a precocious youngster with a lot to say. With a journalist for a father and a writer for a mother, she was exposed to a variety of views on the day's issues. At 13 years of age, her poetry was published in the *Vancouver Province*, but she didn't want to be a poet at first. For years she fought her natural writing inclinations in favour of writing of a more journalistic nature, something that would stand as a challenge for change in areas where young Dorothy saw injustice: poverty, oppression, discrimination, prejudice and other issues stirred Dorothy's heart like no other. In time, she recognized it was through her voice as a poet that she could make the most difference, and her works *Day and Night*, which dealt with the Depression, and *Call My People Home*, which focused on the forced internment of 23,000 Japanese Canadians, were published and subsequently aired on CBC Radio. Along with numerous awards and accolades, Dorothy was awarded the Order of Canada in 1986 and is considered one of Canada's leading poets of the 20th century.

A Free Press

William Fisher Luxton (1844–1907)

In many ways William Fisher Luxton was a Renaissance man. Born in England in 1844, he was just a lad of 11 years when his family immigrated to Canada West (later known as Ontario).

He earned himself a solid education, studying at St. Thomas, and tried his hand at just about everything from farming and teaching to politics. Journalism was Luxton's most ardent calling and, perhaps, where he made his biggest mark when he founded the *Manitoba Free Press* (now the *Winnipeg Free Press*) in 1872. Considered by many "the most influential newspaper in the Prairie West," within two years it was running as a daily with more than 1000 subscribers. William's staff had increased from five to 60 employees, and a new, two-storey building was built to house the operation. William had a fiery pen and after several scathing editorials condemning the railway in one issue and Franco-Manitoban Catholics in another, he was ousted from his seat as owner and editor of the *Free Press* in 1893. Shortly thereafter William started up a rival paper he called the *Daily Nor'Wester*, which he sold in 1896.

FINE ART

The Sound of the Loon

From his triptych image of "Thunder Dancer," "Metamorphosis" and "Thunderbird," to his series on loons, Cree artist Jackson Beardy made waves in the Winnipeg, and later Canadian, art scenes. I remember cooking pork chops for him one day when, during one of his many visits to the Whiteshell, he stopped for dinner at the resort where I worked. Sadly, his life was cut short in 1984 at the age of only 40 years.

Group of Seven Fame

Lionel LeMoine Fitzgerald was born, studied and shared his skills as an art teacher in Winnipeg. His art gained acclaim in a more far-reaching way than just among his immediate colleagues and students when he displayed some of his work at two different venues with works by the Group of Seven in 1930. In 1932, after the death of J.E.H. MacDonald, he was asked to join five of the remaining members in founding the succeeding Canadian Group of Painters. Fitzgerald's 1929 work entitled "Houses" was used as the basis for a gold coin produced by the Royal Canadian Mint in 2003.

A Sculpture Garden

More than 300 bronze sculptures created by Leo Mol are on display at the Leo Mol Sculpture Garden in Assiniboine Park. The garden, which opened in 1992, has been expanded twice to accommodate the sculptures that, for the most part, have been donated by Leo himself. He is also a stained-glass artist. He became an Officer of the Order of Canada in 1989 and was also awarded the Order of Manitoba in 2000.

MUSIC

Prairie Powerhouse

Ah-ha! I can officially say I know someone famous…well, sort of. A brother-in-law on one side of my family and a sister-in-law on the other side both went to school with Burton Cummings (1947–). The famed lead singer of Winnipeg-based The Guess Who led the band from 1965 to 1975, and together they made music history by becoming the first Canadian rock band with a number-one hit in the U.S.—and they had two on the same album with "American Woman" and "No Sugar Tonight." While the group officially split up in 1975, guitarist and composer Randy Bachmann (1943–) left five years earlier and got busy starting up another well-known Canadian band with brother Robbie Bachman (1953–) and fellow Winnipegger Charles Turner (1943–), forming Bachman-Turner Overdrive (or BTO). It is Turner's smooth vocals you hear in the songs "House of the Rising Sun," "Takin' Care of Business" and "Let it Ride."

Bad Brad Roberts

Brad Roberts got his musical start in the mid-1980s as founder of Winnipeg's Blue Note Café's house band Bad Brad Roberts and the St. James Rhythm Pigs. By 1991, the band evolved into the Crash Test Dummies and released its first commercial success in *The Ghosts That Haunt Me*. Brad wrote "Superman's Song"—one of his biggest hit singles—after attending a songwriting workshop with Lyle Lovett. The group's biggest hit was "Mmm Mmm Mmm Mmm," a single from the album *God Shuffled His Feet*. The song made it to the fourth position on the American Billboard Hot 100.

A Voice for Her People

Churchill-born Susan Aglukark has been making waves in the music world since before 1992, but her breakthrough album was released a few years later in 1995. *O Child* and its number-one single "O Siem," propelled her into the national spotlight and resulted in her being the first Inuit performer to have a top-40 hit. She is a three-time Juno Award winner and has played command performances for Canadian prime ministers Jean Chretien and Brian Mulroney, Queen Elizabeth and the president of France, Jacques Chirac. In 2005, she became an Officer of the Order of Canada.

Gospel Great

Contemporary Christian musician Steve Bell hails from the windy city. He is one of Canada's best-known Christian musicians and was awarded the first ever Juno for Best Gospel in 1998.

Multifaceted Musician

From the hosting of the nationally syndicated program *Big Sky Country* to producing and hosting "Rhythms of the Métis" and performing as a voice actor for the Treehouse Network program *Tipi Tales*, Ray St. Germain has just about done it all. Among his many accolades include being named to the Aboriginal Order of Canada and the Order of the Sash and having a plaque on Winnipeg's Aboriginal Wall of Honour.

Which Way You Going?

Stand back you BC braggarts! While Terry Jacks may have migrated westward, he actually hailed from Winnipeg! Born in 1944, he lived in our fair city until well into his teenage years. By the time he moved to Vancouver he had joined a band called the Chessmen. It was when he teamed up with Saskatoon's Susan Pesklevits and added a guitarist and drummer to form the Poppy Family that he really hit his mark as a musician. The group went on to hit the number one spot on Canadian charts and number two on the U.S. billboard charts for their single "Which Way You Goin' Billy?" Terry also worked for a time with the U.S. group the Beach Boys, but his biggest musical accomplishment was the recording "Seasons in the Sun," which was Canada's best selling single ever. The song earned Terry three Juno Awards.

Music Icon
Neil Young moved to Winnipeg as a youngster of about 12 and attended Kelvin High School. A born musician, Neil played whenever he could and wherever he could, and by the time he was 22 he'd joined forces with Buffalo Springfield. Over the years, he has performed as both a solo artist and with various groups, most notably Crosby, Stills, Nash and Young. He's been at it since 1963 and doesn't show any signs of stopping.

Classical Gem
At the age of five (1924), Zara Nelsova performed the cello on stage for the first time in her hometown of Winnipeg, but she later trained in England and played with the London Symphony Orchestra. She performed as a soloist throughout Canada and the U.S., and she was the first North American cellist to play in the Soviet Union. From 1962 until her death in 2002, Zara taught at New York's famous Juilliard School.

Life is a Highway

For Canadian rocker Tom Cochrane, his highway began in the small northern community of Lynn Lake. Tom was born there in 1953 and lived there until he was four years old when his family moved to Ontario.

BALLET AND MUSICAL THEATRE

Royal Winnipeg Ballet

Winnipeg is home to the country's oldest ballet company, the Royal Winnipeg Ballet (founded in 1939) The RWB is the longest continuously operating ballet company in North America. Young dancers dream of a chance to hone their skills as one of the 70 lucky students chosen from across the globe to attend one of the company's fulltime training programs. Among its stars have been David Peregrine and Evelyn Hart.

Fred is for Fun

You know what they say, "Behind every good man is a darn good woman." Writer, musician and singer Fred Penner (1946–) might have all the talent it takes to make it in the children's entertainment world, but it was his wife Odette who really started the ball rolling. The two met in 1977. Odette was a dance choreographer, and she and Fred decided to start a dance and theatre company for children. That's about the time Fred recorded "The Cat Came Back" and the rest, as they say, is history. Since then Fred has toured and performed for youngsters throughout North America.

ENTERTAINMENT

Maverick Manitobans and Their Claims to Fame

Quiet, polite, not ones to blow their own horns—these charac-
teristics are typical for most Canadians, and Manitobans are no
exception. A proud lot, but quietly proud, not wanting to be
stand-offish or seem superior in any way. Still, as a Manitoban,
I had no idea there were so many talented folks from this province in the entertainment industry. Here are just a few notewor-
thy names. Unless otherwise noted, these folks were born, raised
or studied in Winnipeg:

Cordell Barker (1957–)
From *Sesame Street*, where he cut his teeth in 1974 as an appren-
tice animator, to *The Cat Came Back* fame, Cordell has earned
two Oscar nominations during his 25-year career.

Adam Beach (1972–)
Born in Ashern, this Canadian actor of Saulteaux descent had
his hand in the entertainment industry from a young age. While
he started off in music, a role in the 1990 film *Lost in the Barrens*
propelled him into an acting career that has spanned television
and film. Most recently, he starred as Ira Hayes in the 2006
film release *Flags of Our Fathers*.

Steve Braun (1976–)
If you're a fan of serial television shows such as *The Immortal*,
Gilmore Girls or *CSI:NY*, chances are you've caught a glimpse of
this guy.

Len Cariou (1939–)
Len moved his way through an acting career, beginning in
Stratford Ontario and moving on to Broadway, film and televi-
sion. He has appeared on the television shows *Law & Order*,
The West Wing, *The Practice* and *Murder She Wrote* and movies
The Four Seasons, *About Schmidt* and *Flags of Our Fathers*.

Bill Cody (1891–1948)
Mr. Cody acted in a series of B-Western movies.

Richard Condie (1942–)
Educated at the University of Manitoba, Richard didn't enter the world of animation until he was awarded a grant from the Canada Council in 1971. He then produced the animated film *Oh Sure,* and he hasn't looked back since. He's mostly known for his film *The Big Snit,* which garnered him an Oscar and a Genie nomination and earned him 16 international awards.

Ted Corday (1908–1966)
Soap fans should thank Winnipeg for creating one of North America's favourite soap operas, *Days of Our Lives.* This, Corday's final creation, was a long-lasting one as *Days of Our Lives* continues to captivate fans 40 years later.

Deanna Durbin (1921–)
Hollywood actress of the 1930s and 1940s, Deanna signed with Universal Studios, was considered Hollywood's first "teen idol" and earned her way into the hearts of fans across the world and onto a star on Hollywood Boulevard.

Brendan Fehr (1977–)
Brendan started his acting career in 1996 through *CR6,* an Internet soap opera, but it wasn't long before he moved into television and landed a role in *Breaker High.* He was later cast as Michael Guerin in *Roswell.*

Danny Finkleman (1942–)
Since the 1950s, Danny crooned radio listeners with *Finkleman's 45s* on CBC Radio 1. The much-loved show retired with him in 2005.

Ken Finkelman (1946–)
Following in his brother Danny's footsteps into the world of media, Ken wrote and produced a number of individual and series shows for television, most notably *The Newsroom,* where he also starred as the show's news producer George Findlay.

James Freer (1855–1933)

Born in England, James immigrated to Manitoba in 1888. By the early 1890s, inspired by the first films produced by the Lumiere Brothers, he started making films about the prairies, becoming Manitoba's first official filmmaker.

Daniel Gillies (1976–)

Among his many acting roles, Daniel is likely best known for his role in *Spider-Man 2* as John Jameson (son of Peter Parker's boss, J. Jonah Jameson).

Doug Henning (1947–2000)

A master illusionist, Doug was credited with "reviving the magic show" in his own unique way. Instead of being clean-shaven and wearing a top hat and tux, Doug's shaggy mane, bushy moustache and colourful clothes gave his act a modern edge.

Joanna Gleason (1950–)
Joanna hit Broadway in 1977, and her career has continued to skyrocket ever since. Along with television debuts on the shows *ER*, *King of the Hill* and *Diff'rent Strokes*, she's also played in movies including *Hannah and her Sisters*, *Mr. Holland's Opus* and *The Wedding Planner*.

Tom Jackson (1948–)
A young Tom spent several years living on the streets of Winnipeg, and perhaps it was this experience that added depth to the characters he played on shows such as *North of 60*. Aside from his fame as an actor, singer and musician, he is a much-loved philanthropist who for almost 20 years has worked to raise money for food banks across the country.

Monty Hall (1921–)
Monty is best known for *Let's Make a Deal*, the game show he hosted and helped develop. The show ran for 14 full seasons (1963–77) and has continued to run in various incarnations up until 2006.

Tina Keeper (1962–)
Of *North of 60* fame, Tina traded in entertainment for the political stage when she was elected as Liberal Member of Parliament for Churchill in 2006.

Paul Maxwell (1921–91)
Paul made his mark on British television, most notably for his role in the long-running soap opera *Coronation Street*.

Tom McCamus (1955–)
Tom is best known for his role as Mason Eckhart on the television show *Mutant X*.

Guy Maddin (1956–)
A prolific Canadian filmmaker with more than 30 movies to his credit, Guy does everything from writing scripts to acting, producing and directing. He has also won several awards including an Emmy for *Dracula: Pages from a Virgin's Diary* (2002).

John Paizs (1958–)

This fella's got quite the resume. Along with a long list of directing and producing credits including the television series *Kids in the Hall* and *The Adventures of Shirley Holmes*, he's apparently also acted in adult films.

Anna Paquin (1982–)

Although she was raised in New Zealand, Anna was born in Winnipeg so we can, technically, call her one of our own. Anna hit the big screen early with a 1993 role in the movie *The Piano*. Her introduction to the movie industry earned her an Academy Award for Best Supporting Actress. More recently she acted in the series of *X-Men* movies and in 2006 completed filming and producing the movie *Blue State*.

Douglas Rain (1928–)

Remember *2001:A Space Odyssey* and its sequel, *2010:The Year We Make Contact*? The voice of Hal was played by Winnipeg-born Douglas Rain.

Natalie Reid (1985–)

This Transcona-born actress, singer and model is most famous for her celebrity look-alike stints as Paris Hilton. She's also posed for *Playboy Magazine*, one of only four Winnipeggers to do so.

Donnelly Rhodes (1937–)

Donnelly is known for the role he played as Dr. Cottell on *Battlestar Galactica*, but diehard *Young and the Restless* fans might remember him in the role of Phillip Chancellor II.

Bill Richardson (1955–)

Writer and broadcaster, Bill is likely best known as host of *The Roundup* on CBC Radio 1.

David Steinberg (1942–)

David has directed several award-winning sitcoms, such as *Seinfeld*, *Mad About You* and *Friends*.

Nia Vardalos (1962–)

This Winnipeg-born Greek goddess was catapulted into international fame when *My Big Fat Greek Wedding*, which she wrote and acted in as the main character, hit the big screen. It was the fifth highest grossing movie of 2002, earning $241,438,208. Needless to say, Nia has several other irons in the fire, including starring roles in *A Wilderness of Monkeys*, which is being directed by Tom Hanks for Universal Pictures, and *My Life in Ruins*, again directed by Tom Hanks and Gary Goetzman for Hanks' Playtone Productions.

Catherine Wreford (1980–)

She's a dancer, singer and Jeff Goldbloom's wife, not necessarily in that order. In the last couple of years, the young actress has appeared in at least six movies including the soon to be released *Pittsburgh*, which also stars her husband.

LAW AND CRIME

Westward Ho!

"Go west, young man, and grow up with the country."
Although this quote is attributed to Indiana newspaperman
John B.L. Soule in an editorial he wrote back in 1851 encouraging young men to venture west, the sentiment applied equally to
pioneers putting down stakes in Canada. Young, ambitious fellas would leave their homes in the east or even Europe in search
of making their mark out west. Policing these newly founded,
largely male communities was likely more than a bit of a challenge. And even though Manitoba is a fairly peaceful place to
be, we've had our share of dirty deeds to deal with.

Common Crimes

Based on 2005 Stats Canada statistics, crime dropped overall
throughout Canada by about five percent. But the picture isn't
all rosy. Most of that drop was attributed to less serious crimes
and homicide; attempted murder and other serious crimes were
at or past previous rates. In fact, the homicide rate in 2005 was
the highest it had been since 1996. Here's how Manitoba
stacked up against the rest of the country.

Criminal Offence	Canada	Manitoba
Homicide	658	49
Assault	234,729	14,755
Sexual Assault	23,303	1318
Robbery	28,669	2007
Breaking & Entering	259,521	13,218
Car Theft	160,100	14,200

Youth and Crime

Youth aged 12 to 17 are committing crimes at an alarming rate.
Perhaps most disturbing is the province's murder stats, which
are stacked up higher than other provinces with considerably
larger populations. In 2005, there were 2,566,450 youth in this
age group throughout Canada. Manitoba's population was
101,865, and there were 9 murders. On the other hand,
Ontario, with a population of 1,006,334, saw 12 murders in
this age grouping. Here are a few more statistics:

Criminal Offence	Canada	Manitoba
Homicide	65	9
Assault	29,417	1847
Sexual Assault	2212	85
Robbery	4070	236
Breaking & Entering	13,651	1111
Car Theft	5163	489

Long Arm of the Law

Keeping the peace in any community is always a priority, and once a settlement had opened up at the junction of the Red and Assiniboine Rivers, the next task was to set down the laws of the land and establish a police force.

- The first written laws for the area were produced by the Hudson's Bay Company in 1835

- Captain Frank Villiers, a member of the 2nd Quebec Rifles, established the settlement's first Mounted Constabulary Force (MCF) in 1870. The new police force started out with 10 of Villiers' colleagues and 10 local men. These 20 men were expected to enforce the law throughout the entire province.

- Break the law, and you'd be locked up in the province's first penitentiary—a makeshift warehouse built in Lower Fort Garry in 1858 served the purpose from 1871 to 1877

- The first police chief for the city of Winnipeg was John S. Ingram. He was appointed on February 23, 1874

- Winnipeg currently has two police departments: the Winnipeg City Police and the Winnipeg Parks Police. With more than 900 residential parks and 12 regional parks occupying 4152 hectares of land, a separate force had to be established to keep them safe. Twelve members are assigned to this constabulary.

Weird and Wacky Laws

A quick perusal of old community bylaws often makes for interesting conversation. Here are a few tidbits from across the province.

- Get caught driving faster than 30 kilometres per hour down a back lane in Winnipeg, and you'll get a ticket. The back lane speeding bylaw was first enacted in 1978 and updated in 2002.

☞ Back in December 1955, a new Carman bylaw restricted folks from tossing household ashes in the street. Folks caught doing so would receive a $2 fine. The bylaw was either unnecessary or angered the wrong people because it was repealed a few months later.

☞ Since 1979, train engineers were restricted from blowing their whistle in 20 various locations listed in the bylaw. Hmmm, that engineer definitely needs to be on the ball.

☞ To ensure youngsters (and their dads) didn't get carried away playing on those gas-powered model vehicles, the town of Morden passed a bylaw in 2003 restricting their use within 300 metres of a residence. Powered airplanes and helicopters were also banished to outside town limits.

☞ Entrepreneurial types in Winkler are welcome to set up shop in their homes with a few limitations—they can't clutter the outside of their home with displays, storage materials or anything that would tip off other residents that a business was being housed there.

☞ The town of Beausejour allows snowmobile traffic in town from October 15 to April 15. The only streets that are off limits are Park Avenue and First Street North.

- You can not drive a snowmobile inside Morden's town limits unless a snowstorm has shut down the highways.

- Since a bylaw was passed in 1993, door-to-door sales people in Neepawa must have a valid business licence. The only folks exempt from this rule are farmers selling their produce at market or magazine and newspaper peddlers. The fresh fruit truck from the Okanagan, on the other hand, better have a licence close at hand or the powers that be won't approve.

- Since 1950, it has been against the law in Carman to sell "newspapers, magazines or any other type of publication on town streets or the surrounding highways."

- In 2001, Carman passed a bylaw allowing townsfolk to shoot crows and grackles. It seems that the feathered fowl were becoming quite the nuisance.

- A 2004 bylaw in Neepawa mandates that house numbers be a minimum of 12 centimetres in height and be a contrasting colour to the building.

- Better keep your yard neat if you're a homeowner in Morden. Residents are expected to keep their lawns nicely mowed, and they can't litter their yards with appliances and cars strewn about willy nilly.

- Placing a number that measures at least 10 centimetres in heigh on the front of your home was made law in Morden in 2004.

- If you lived in Neepawa back in 1898, when it was still considered the Northwest Territories, and an animal wandered onto and damaged your property, you were to blame. That's because properties were to be surrounded by a fence, which, depending on where you lived, had to meet specific requirements.

- At some point in Winnipeg's history, it was against the law to hit a sidewalk with a metal object.

- Youngsters in Churchill better adhere to the town's curfew laws or they'll find themselves and their folks in hot water with the authorities. The graduated curfew requires kids aged 11 years and younger be at home or with a parent by 10:00 PM, those aged 12 to 15 years by 11:00 PM and ages 16 and 17 by midnight. Youth repeatedly disregarding this curfew are fined $100 and expected to work community service hours. Their parents, on the other hand, find themselves back at school taking parenting classes.

- One source states Churchill youngsters can't wear furry costumes on Halloween to prevent them from being mistaken for a baby seal. After all, that's polar bear country.

WINNIPEG'S WORST OFFENDERS

Making Headlines

We've all heard our parents say that back in their day things were different. You didn't have to worry about your kids playing outside or making their way to a friend's house like you do today. But for about two years, 1945–47, parents of boys in their early teens were panic-stricken after a series of rapes evolved into what city police were calling "The Pervert Murders." In the end, the former army private Michael Angelo Vescio was sentenced to death for the rape and murder of 13-year-old George Smith. He was also charged with the rape and murder of 13-year-old Roy Ewan McGregor and earlier sexual assaults of three boys ranging in age from 11 to 14 years. First nicknamed the "sex maniac from Fort Rouge," he was later bestowed with the dubious title of "Winnipeg's greatest sex murderer."

DID YOU KNOW?

The practice of using an army mine detector to uncover bullets at a crime scene was the brainchild of the Winnipeg City Police Department and was first used in "The Pervert Murders." The technique was eventually adopted by "every police department in North America" and even introduced to the F.B.I.

Unsolved Mystery

One minute five-year-old Julia Johnson was bouncing a ball and waiting for a friend to return home from school, and the next she had vanished. That was 1928. The police searched extensively, conducted interviews and grilled suspects, but nothing was uncovered until 1937 when a machinist named Wilfred Adams set out to dismantle the boiler in a vacant building behind where the girl and her family once lived. When he cut open the boiler's combustion chamber, he discovered the mummified remains of little Julia. The case was reopened, but the questions surrounding her death have never been answered.

Walking Oxymoron

One would think someone lecturing on the virtues of temperance lived a life where morality was somewhat central to their way of thinking. But for Jack Krafchenko, also known as Bloody Jack, handing out bad cheques while on the temperance speaking circuit landed him an 18-month prison sentence. He managed a successful escape, padded his pockets with $2500 he stole in a hold-up, and travelled the seven seas, robbing banks and moving on from place to place until he returned to Manitoba in 1906. From then until the end of 1913, Krafchenko continued robbing banks and moving between Manitoba and the U.S. to escape authorities. During the December 3, 1913, robbery of the Bank of Montreal in Plum Coulee, Krafchenko reportedly turned after leaving the bank and shot the manager dead. Krafchenko's trial ran from March 18 to April 9, he was found guilty of murder (and had already admitted to the robbery) and was executed on July 9.

Botched Bank Robberies

Should there ever be a serial television shows highlighting the world's stupidest criminals, the lads involved in this 1944 case might land themselves their 15 minutes of fame. Two newly released Stony Mountain inmates, Frank Shura (32) and Arthur Frederick Evans (37), started brainstorming with William Dacko (24) and Leonard Leroy Peterson (23) about the possibility of pulling of a bank robbery. Joe Wyzrob (also known as Joe Houstin, age unknown) was approached by the group, but he only agreed to loan them his car for the job. In a weird quirk of fate, as the would-be bank robbers were getting out of the car near the targeted bank, Evans bumped Peterson and the gun in his pocket discharged, shooting Wyzrob in the chest. Evans raced Wyzrob to the hospital while the other three culprits raced to the nearby river to ditch the weapon. Of course, they needed to regroup, get another getaway vehicle and plan for their next attempt. Romanuk decided to back out of the deal, and Shura replaced him with another fellow only known as Lanky. On May 29, they thought that they had got it all worked out only to turn the corner and see a police constable at the bank's front door. Again, their robbery had to be postponed. On June 1, they went to a different bank convinced that it was the day only to spot yet another beat cop and a cruiser with a couple more just down the block. At this point, one would think the light bulb would go on and these fellas would have realized this wasn't going to end well, but they persevered and the next day made another attempt. This time the would-be robbers actually made it into the bank, guns drawn and began by moving everyone on the scene to a corner of the bank. Bank manager Hugh Allingham and another employee, Samuel Caughey, weren't going along without a fight. Caughey ended up with a shotgun blast to his face, and the three robbers fled. All the perpetrators were eventually rounded up and by July a trial found Shura, Evans and Dacko guilty of Caughey's murder and sentenced to life in prison while Peterson got 12 years for manslaughter.

Bumbling Criminal

From his first attempts at burglary, it was clear John Nankerville wasn't going to make a lot of money. His first trip to the penitentiary was back in 1885, but it seemed that the jail had a revolving door for him, and he was incarcerated many times thereafter. That all ended in 1896 when things really started going badly. Reports indicate that he tried to rob the Electric Street Railway Company by shooting Superintendent Thomas Glenwright, but he missed (thankfully, I'm sure) and fled the scene. The story was written up in the media, and William Smith, an old cell mate of John's, read the account. Thinking it sounded like John's history of botched robberies, he met with his old buddy over drinks and heard the whole story. John then started having second thoughts about spilling the beans to another con, so he sought William out and shot him in the head. Three bullets didn't kill him, nor did being buried in the snow. William managed to drag himself to a nearby doorstop; the police were called; William was shipped off to the hospital; and he miraculously survived the whole ordeal. John was charged with attempted murder and spent the rest of his life in jail.

Short Order Sentencing
From a justice perspective, the case of John Nankerville was nothing short of extraordinary. Less than 12 hours after John attempted to kill fellow inmate William Smith, Nankerville was in a preliminary hearing. He faced trial within a month and was convicted shortly thereafter. Talk about moving quickly.

From California to Winnipeg

Manitoba's most notorious serial killer was the 13th criminal to meet his maker at the end of a hangman's noose in Winnipeg's Vaughn Street Goal. It was a cold day in January 1928, when Earl Leonard Nelson's trail of rape, death and carnage came to an end in the windy city. But his life began in the much warmer climes of California. He was born in San Francisco on May 12, 1897, and he had been in and out of state mental hospitals for attempted assaults and other crimes. His trail of death and destruction as the Gorilla Strangler began in Philadelphia on October 18, 1925. Mrs. Olla McCoy was Earl's first victim. From there, the Gorilla Strangler criss-crossed the U.S. several times, leaving a wake of 24 dead women before landing in Winnipeg. On June 9, 1927, Lila Cowan was found dead. The next day offered up a second victim in the person of Emily Patterson. Earl was captured trying to leave Manitoba on June 13, 1927. He was tried and found guilty of the murder of Emily Patterson, but was suspected in a total of 26 rapes and murders (some say even more) that took place over less than two years, making him the most prolific serial killer of the day.

DRUGS, BOOZE AND ALL THINGS NAUGHTY

Legal Liquor

At 18 years of age, Manitobans are granted all the rights and privileges of adulthood. They can vote, sign their own apartment leases and consume alcohol. According to the Canadian Centre on Substance Abuse, Manitoba, Alberta and Québec are the only three provinces with a legal drinking age of 18, with the rest of the country opting for 19. Manitoba's legal drinking age was adopted on August 1, 1970. Before that you had to be 21 before indulging in libations.

A Crowning Achievement

Gimli is home to a whisky fit for a king. In fact, it was in honour of the first Canadian Royal Tour in 1939, by then reining monarchs King George VI and Queen Elizabeth, that Crown Royal whisky was created. The idea was the brainchild of Samuel Bronfman, who was president of the Montreal-based Seagram Company at the time. He thought it would be a great treat to produce a quality whisky and package it in a crown-shaped bottle. For that extra special royal touch, the bottle was then wrapped in a purple cloth bag before being boxed. Voila! The king of spirits was born.

The historic recipe of 10,000 bushels of grain and 6 million gallons of water is apparently still followed to produce its required 1000 barrels of the spirit daily. With Gimli located on the shores of Lake Winnipeg—the 13th largest freshwater source in the world—the location is prime. Today, Gimli's is the only distillery to make the product.

High Society

Crown Royal whisky lovers who enjoy "the finer things in life" can become members of the Society of the Crown. As members, they can purchase everything from company-branded boxers to polo shirts, hoodies, caps, engraved glassware and even personalized labels.

DID YOU KNOW?

The word *whisky* is Gaelic for "water of life." It can be spelled two ways—ending with "y" or "ey." Canadians and Scots prefer the older spelling, which excludes the "e," while the Americans and Irish spell it with an "ey."

Still a Sin

Until a recent vote, the rural municipalities of Stanley, Hanover and Sifton were considered "dry" or alcohol-free communities. An article by the Manitoba Hotel Association, dated October 27, 2006, reported the recent vote that saw the rural municipalities of Stanley and Sifton lift the ban on alcohol in its communities. After a tight vote, 1320 against 1291, the rural municipality of Hanover did not revoke its dry status.

HOCKEY

Winnipeg Jets

Founded in 1972, the Winnipeg Jets spent their first seven years as members of the World Hockey Association (WHA) before making the leap into the National Hockey League (NHL). The team was part of the city until 1996 when it was bought out and moved to Phoenix to become the Phoenix Coyotes.

The Winnipeg Jets held their own, for the most part, in the WHA. They were considered one of the best teams in hockey, NHL and WHA, of the era. In fact, the team even won an Avco Cup championship in their final season in the league, 1978–79, in a game against upcoming hockey great, Wayne Gretzky with the Edmonton Oilers. During its NHL years, the team struggled to make the playoffs. The best year on record was the 1984–85 season, when the team won 43 of their 80 scheduled games and finished with 96 points and second place in the old Smythe division. Regardless of its incarnation, the team did have its heroes. Among them were Hall of Famers Bobby Hull (inducted 1983) and Dale Hawerchuck (inducted 2001). Here are a few of the former Winnipeg Jets notable records:

- ☛ Teemu Selanne made it into the Winnipeg Jets record books in his rookie year, the 1992–93 season, after scoring the most goals of any Jet in a season (76) and accruing the most points in a season (132)

- ☛ Phil Housley, also in the 1992–93 season, scored a team record with the most assists in a season (79) and the most points by a defenceman in a season (97)

- ☛ Leave it to good-old Tie Domi to set this record for the Winnipeg Jets. In the 1993–94 season he accrued the most penalty minutes with 347

DID YOU  KNOW?

Diehard fans raised more than $13 million in an effort to save their hockey team, the Winnipeg Jets, from being sold. When their efforts failed, the money raised was donated to charity.

Manitoba Moose

The American Hockey League team, the Manitoba Moose, first hung up a shingle in Winnipeg during the 2001–02 season, five years after the city lost their NHL team, the Winnipeg Jets, to Phoenix. Since their arrival, during which time the AHL has admittedly undergone some structural changes where teams have been moved from one division to another, the Moose have held their own in the middle of the pack. Their best seasons to date were the 2004–05 and 2005–06 seasons, when they won 44 of their 80 scheduled games, earning 98 and 100 points respectively.

Brandon Wheat Kings

The Brandon Wheat Kings were established in Brandon a year after the Western Hockey League's reformation and name change in 1966, just in time to compete in the 1967–68 season. Since then the team has, for the most part, managed a strong showing when compared with other teams in the league. For three seasons running, 1976–79, the team placed first in the east and won the divisional championship in 1978–79. They had another three-year run with first place finishes, 1994–97, and again won the championship in the 1995–96 season. They won first place in 2001–02, 2002–03 and 2004–05, but winning the Memorial Cup has thus far eluded them. Twenty teams were listed on the 2006–07 rosters, and the Brandon Wheat Kings player highlights from past seasons include the following (Source: Brandon Wheat Kings):

- ☛ Ray Ferraro scored 108 goals during the 1983–84 regular season play—a record that stands to date.

- ☛ During the 1983–84 regular season, Cam Plante racked up 118 assists, another record that has yet to crumble.

- ☛ Netminder Tyler Plante maintained a best goals-against average at 2.56 and the most shutouts (six) during the 2004–05 regular season play.

- ☛ Goalie George Maneluk managed 2133 saves during the 1987–88 regular season play—a record even Plante couldn't better.

- ☛ Goalies Dave McLelland and Glen Hanlon played 65 games each in the 1971–72 and 1976–77 seasons respectively. That's the highest number of games played by a single goalie during regular season play.

Small-town Heroes

It's not uncommon for cities the size of Winnipeg to produce a handful of athletes of NHL calibre, but come from a small town and make it to the big leagues, and you're a star forever. Manitoba has several communities boasting homegrown talent. Here are just a few of the many big names:

Town	Player	Drafted	Years
Brandon	Sheldon Kennedy	1989	7
Carman	Eddie "The Eagle" Belfour	1990	to present
Churchill	Jordin Tootoo	2001	to present
Eriksdale	"Terrible Ted" Green	1960	19
Foxwarren	Ron Low	1970	14
Foxwarren	Pat Falloon	1991	9
Foxwarren	Mark Wotton	1992	4
Glenboro	Mel "Sudden Death" Hill	1938	9
Portage la Prairie	Rick Blight	1975	8
Poplar Point	Bryan Hextall	1936	13
Poplar Point	Bryan Hextall Jr.	1962	14
Brandon	Ron Hextall	1986	12
Flin Flon	Bobby Clarke	1969	15
Stony Mountain	Walter "Babe" Pratt	1935	13
Riverton	Reggie Leach	1970	13
Russell	Mervyn "Red" Dutton	1921	15
Russell	Theoren Fleury	1987	16
St. Boniface	Butch Goring	1969	16
Steinbach	Ian White	2003	to present
Winkler	Dustin Penner	2005	to present

Northern Champion

Jordin Tootoo made Manitoban and Canadian history as the first Inuit player to be drafted into the NHL. He was drafted in 2001 by the Nashville Predators and played his first regular season game on October 9, 2003. He scored his first NHL goal shortly thereafter in a game against the Atlanta Thrashers on October 23 of the same year.

Top of His Class

Winnipeg-born Terry Sawchuck first caught the eye of NHL scouts at the age of 14 and by 17 the goalie had signed his first contract for the Detroit Red Wings farm team in Omaha. Despite a childhood injury that restricts him from bending his arm, he is thought of by many as the greatest goalie of all time. In 1998, he was ranked as ninth among the NHL's top 50 players of all time by the *Hockey News*.

DID YOU  KNOW?

St. Boniface native Modere Fernand "Mud" Bruneteau is credited with ending the longest game in NHL playoff history. As a member of the Detroit Red Wings, he scored the winning goal against the Montréal Maroons on March 24, 1936, at the 16.30 mark of the sixth overtime period. The final score was 1-0. Talk about a nailbiter!

Hockey Highlights

The Winnipeg Falcons hockey team made provincial history in March 1921 when they became the first Manitoba team to win the National Cup, defeating the Stratford Midgets by a score of 7–2.

Art on Ice

If you travel through Boissevain, you're likely to notice the vast array (20 at last count) of outdoor murals. Among them is a heritage scene of a group of youngsters playing pond hockey with little more than a few sticks, frozen cow patties for pucks and Eaton's catalogues for shin guards. The scene speaks of the importance of hockey in prairie culture. Manitoba has produced many hockey greats.

FOOTBALL AND RUGBY

Go Blue!

Technically speaking, Winnipeg has been cheering on its football heroes since 1880. Back then, of course, the team wasn't the Blue Bombers—they didn't officially make an appearance on the scene until 1930 under the leadership of Dick Mahoney. In 1880, it was the Winnipeg Rugby Football Club that entertained fans on warm, summer nights. This club, also known as the "Winnipegs," laid the foundation for their future incarnation as the Blue Bombers when they amalgamated with other teams in Manitoba's Rugby Union.

Unlike Winnipeg's hockey legacy, the city's football team has left an indelible mark on the history of the sport in Canada. Here is a sampling of Bomber trivia:

☛ In 1935, the Blue Bombers were the first team west of Ontario to win the Grey Cup

- The team acquired the name "Blue Bombers" after sports writer Vince Leah called them "the Blue Bombers of Western Football"

- The Winnipeg Stadium, built in 1953, was nicknamed "The House that Jack Built." The moniker was a tribute to Jack Jacobs—an Native quarterback from Holdenville, Oklahoma. His incredible talent drew so many fans that he was credited for filling the Osborne Stadium to capacity, creating the need for a larger venue.

- As of the 2005–06 season, the team had garnered 10 Grey Cups (1935, 1939, 1941, 1958, 1959, 1961, 1962, 1984, 1988, 1990)

- The 1961 Grey Cup faceoff between the Blue Bombers and the Hamilton Tiger-Cats was a real nailbiter. It was the first and only Grey Cup final to date to be decided in overtime.

- Poor weather was the culprit, bringing a halt to the December 1, 1962 Grey Cup game 9:29 minutes before the end of the fourth quarter. The remainder of the game had to be played the following day, and the end result saw the Bombers victorious over Toronto by a score of 28–27. Incidentally, the 9:29 minutes of the game completed the following day didn't make a difference to the score.

BASEBALL FEVER

Winnipeg Goldeyes

Winnipeg welcomed a minor league baseball team for a second time in 1994 when the Winnipeg Goldeyes, the second Winnipeg baseball team to use the name, played their first season in the Northern League under the ownership and presidency of current mayor Sam Katz. Since its reincarnation, the team has earned one championship (in its inaugural year) and seven division titles (1994, 1997, 1998, 1999, 2001, 2002, 2003). Compare the Goldeyes' 2006 stats against the rest of the league, and it's clear the team has some serious star power:

☛ Winnipeg has two names in the top 10 when it comes to batting: Fehlandt Lentini with an average of .325 and an RBI of 49 and Jimmy Hurst with an average of .307 and an RBI of 78

☛ Goldeyes pitchers are a force to be reckoned with. Luis Villarreal leads the division with an ERA of 2.71. Josh Beshears is in sixth spot with 3.25 and Ben Moore in seventh with 3.30.

☛ Jimmy Hurst ranks third in the league with 18 home runs

☛ Fehlandt Lentini leads the league in stolen bases with 57

☛ Fehlandt Lentini also ranks among the best in hits (second with 136), doubles (second with 32) and triples (leading the league with 13)

☛ Josh Beshears comes in fifth in the wins category with 10

☛ Josh Kite ranks fifth in saves with 12

☛ Jimmy Hurst and Fehlandt Lentini rank third and fourth in slugging percentage with .531 and .507 respectively

☛ Jimmy Hurst and Fehlandt Lentini also rank in the top five for runs scored with Lentini in second place with 93 and Hurst in fourth with 74

☛ Fehlandt Lentini is second in the league for extra-base hits with 51

☛ As a team, the Goldeyes rank second in team batting and team pitching with a .274 in the batting category and 3.80 in ERAs. They were bettered both times by Fargo-Moorhead.

DID YOU KNOW?

Before the Winnipeg Goldeyes run in 1954 to 1964 and again in 1994 to the present, the windy city did host another Northern League baseball team. The Winnipeg Maroons played for 40 years between 1902 and 1942.

Big League Bound

Anola might be a hamlet with a population of not more than 200 people, but it was home to Corey Koskie. Born in 1973, Corey was drafted to the Minnesota Twins in 1998 and currently plays as third baseman for the Milwaukee Brewers.

Canada Day Homerun

Since 1951, the town of Clearwater has celebrated Canada Day with an annual baseball tournament, which includes seniors to junior boys, junior girls and the "Mixed Liniment League" teams.

Manitoba Baseball Hall of Fame

I admit it. Aside from watching my kids play, I have not been much of a baseball fan. But after discovering that a Manitoba Baseball Hall of Fame existed in Morden and doing a quick perusal of their website, my interest in the sport in the province was piqued.

The idea for establishing the museum came about in 1996. A charitable organization was formed the following year, and by 1999, the Manitoba Baseball Hall of Fame was established at the Morden Recreation Centre. At last count there were 166 inductees—all Manitobans who loved the sport and contributed to its growth in some way, from the minors to Manitoba's many senior leagues. As well, group photos representing major teams, special teams and community teams that have made their mark on the province's baseball story are also on display.

ICE AND SNOW

Colourful Curler

Eddie "The Wrench" Werenich is thought to have made curling history as the first curler to have earned $1,000,000 on the ice. He was born in Benito in 1947.

Snow Surfing

Forget a claim to local fame, Beausejour's boast is worldwide. The town's Canadian Power Toboggan Championships Raceplex is the site of the oldest continually running snowmobile race in the world. The idea for the event was registered by the Beausejour Lion's Club in 1962, and by 1963 a makeshift course had been set up at a local schoolyard. There's been no looking back ever since. In 1967 the Canadian Power Toboggan Championship (CPTC) constructed an oval at Beausejour's Centennial Park, and by 1972 interest in the event had grown to such a degree that crowds that year were estimated at about 25,000. Today, the annual championship includes races in the professional, semi-professional, junior, women's and vintage events.

INSPIRATIONAL ATHLETES

Marathon of Hope

Terrence Stanley Fox (1958–1981)

Winnipeg-born Terry Fox might have thought he had a career in water sports. An avid swimmer and diver, Terry competed regularly and earned himself a wide assortment of medals for his efforts. But his biggest athletic and personal challenge came three years after his right leg was amputated just above his right knee in 1977 because of osteosarcoma, a type of bone cancer. It was then, at the age of 20, that the young athlete embarked on his now-famous Marathon of Hope—a fundraising venture that, had he finished, would have seen him run across the country from St. John's, Newfoundland to Victoria, BC. He set off on his journey on April 12, 1980, but had to end his cross-country quest in Thunder Bay—143 days and 5373 kilometres into his race. While the cancer that had spread to his lungs had forced him to quit his run, his strength of spirit continues to this day as communities across Canada continue to work toward raising money for cancer research by hosting annual Terry Fox runs every September.

A Water Wonderland

A plethora of lakes makes Manitoba a water-lover's paradise.
Swimming, jet skiing, windsurfing, fishing, rowing, canoeing,
kayaking…the list of recreational possibilities is only really limited by one's imagination. One place where Manitoba really
excels, when it comes to summer sport, is in waterskiing. The
father–son team of Ian and Bruce Reid set the bar for anyone
hoping to make it big on the waterskiing scene. Ian spent at least
30 years dedicated to the sport, earned himself a number of provincial awards and, in 1953, worked to establish the Selkirk
Seals, the province's first waterski club. Although Ian never competed nationally, his mark on the sport was far from over.

Enter young Bruce.

Bruce inherited his father's enthusiasm for water sports and
excelled in waterskiing. In fact on his induction, the Manitoba
Sports Hall of Fame & Museum says this of the superstar: "No
Manitoba waterskier can boast the illustrious career of Alexander
Bruce Reid; none had gone as far before him and it is unlikely
that any will surpass his accomplishments in the near future."

Bruce captured provincial and national championships in several waterskiing categories, including figures, slalom, jumping and overall. He competed internationally from 1973 to 1983, placing sixth overall at the 1981 World Championships.

Ian and Bruce were both inducted into the Manitoba Sports Hall of Fame & Museum in 1986, making them the first father and son pair to receive the honour.

ROADSIDE ATTRACTIONS

Mascot Madness
Manitoba is a veritable breeding ground for roadside attractions. Pass by any number of communities, and it's almost as if they're competing for the largest, most obscure roadside mascot.

Yellowhead It
A trip through Manitoba via the Yellowhead Highway offers a lot more in the way of scenery than its southern counterpart, the Trans-Canada. Rivalling for your attention are a number of roadside attractions that are so interesting, they can't help but say something about the communities they represent.

Russell
This town is the home of hockey great Theoren Fleury, the Beef and Barley Festival and Arthur the Bull. The well-loved mascot came to be in 1972. In 2001, it inherited the name Arthur, honouring Beef and Barley Festival founder and one-time mayor Art Kinney.

Minnedosa
If you aren't looking for it, you could conceivably drive by and not notice Minnedosa. If you really pay attention, you might catch a glimpse of their 5-metre-long canvasback duck. Suspended overhead at the junction of Highways 10, 16 and 16A, the mascot was created in 2001 as a millennium project and in honour of the fact the canvasback duck uses the area for summer breeding grounds.

Neepawa

This town seems to attract a lot of great things: an abundance of lilies, legendary literary folk and purple martins. In the case of the latter, Neepawa's roadside attraction might be a serious drawing card. Boasting the "World's Tallest and Largest Purple Martin Colony," the eight-storey tower supports 24 large and three extra-large purple martin houses. You can catch sight of these houses as you travel east out of Neepawa on the Yellowhead.

Gladstone

How can you ever be sad when you live in a place named Gladstone? To make sure that "glad" spirit is caught by folks driving past town, the community erected Mr. Happy Rock. The mascot was built atop a small visitors' booth in 1993. Face it, you can't get away with a poor disposition in this town, visitor or not!

Portage la Prairie

This central city boasts two roadside attractions. The "World's Largest Coke Can" was constructed out of an old water tower on the western outskirts of the city, and a large wood-carved grey owl sits atop a fencepost to the north of town.

Trans-Canada Bound

Yes, it's true. Travel through Manitoba on the Trans-Canada Highway, and there's not much to see, so the few roadside attractions scattered along the way are a welcome sight.

Virden
The town is a little ways off the Trans-Canada, but Virden's oil derrick is a must-see. Besides, by the time you make it anywhere near the town you'll need something to break up the monotony! Apparently there is oil in them thar' fields. In fact, the community calls itself the "Oil Capital of Manitoba."

Oak Lake
Back on the right road again, Oak Lake salutes Manitoba's pioneers with an ox and cart. Erected in 1986, the statue is said to be visible from Highway 1.

St. Francis Xavier
A great white horse greets folks passing the junction of highways 1 and 26, near the town of St. Francis Xavier.

Winnipeg
There are at least half a dozen various mascot-type roadside attractions around town. There's Big Blue the Bear, a salute to the Blue Bombers no doubt, who is just one of 62 such bear

sculptures along Broadway Avenue. (These bears were part of a fundraising effort for the CancerCare Manitoba Foundation.) There's also Winnie the Bear, a salute to the Winnipeg inspiration for Winnie the Pooh. Winnipeg also has its own ox cart, as well as a dala horse, a buffalo and a salute to tighty-whities (a statue of starched underwear).

Transcona
When I was a youngster, this suburb was loosely connected to the big city of Winnipeg by one main artery. Today, it's a thriving community that's expanded so far to the east it seems like just a matter of time before it connects up with what used to be longstanding farming communities. Folks living there haven't changed though and are a welcoming lot: the neighbourhood greeter stands, hat in hand, to bid visitors a good day.

North to...Hudson Bay?

Communities in northern Manitoba are home to some of the province's oldest and most intriguing roadside mascots.

The Pas.
The 7-metre-tall sculpture of a trapper waves visitors into town, holding a sign of the town's name just in case you forgot where you were. The trapper was erected in honour of the town's Trapper's Festival.

Dauphin
Amisk (the Cree word for beaver) was built as the town's mascot in 1967. The 5-metre-tall beaver was built as a Canadian Centennial project.

Roblin
This town calls itself the "Jewel of the Parkland," and to ensure folks are aware of the distinction, Roblin erected a large jewel as a millennium project. At its base is a time capsule, and the sculpture sits in the town's Millennium Park.

Flin Flon
Josiah Flintabbatey Flonatin, the fictional character from the 1905 James Muddock novel *The Sunless City*, has made his mark on the northern city of Flin Flon in more ways than one. The city's name was derived from the main novel's character—and it's believed to be the only city in the world to be named after a science fiction character. In some ways the city exudes this fanciful nature. In honour of this character, cartoonist Al Capp, of Lil' Abner fame, created the town's over 7-metre-tall mascot affectionately known as Flinty back in the 1960s. True to the novel's plot, you can also see a sculpture of Flinty riding a submarine and suspended in the air at Flinty's Submarine Park.

Sifton
A spinning wheel stands proud atop a stone and concrete cairn as a salute to the wool industry that once had its home there, as well as to Willard McPhedrain, founder of the internationally renowned Mary Maxim Company.

Selkirk
This community has two roadside attractions: a Red River ox cart, built in 1971 to celebrate the town's heritage, and Chuck the Channel Cat, built in 1986 as a tourist attraction and a dedication to "Good Sport and Good Fishing."

Winnipeg Beach
The Whispering Giant greets visitors near the information booth. The 11-metre-tall, carved red cedar sculpture was built as a tribute to the Ojibwa, Assiniboine and Cree Nations.

Thompson
The King Miner (or Mighty Miner) measures 4 metres tall and was built in 1981 as part of the town's 25th anniversary celebrations.

Gimli
In a salute to its Icelandic heritage, a 4.6-metre-tall Viking, built in 1967, stands on Second Avenue as if overseeing the business of the day.

Inwood
The town is in natural denning area for garter snakes, so Sam and Sara were a natural choice when Inwood was deciding to build a roadside attraction. Sam, who measures 7.6 metres, and Sara, who measures almost 8.8 metres, are the pair of garter snakes basking on a granite and limestone foundation just across from the town's hotel.

Petersfield
A statue of a mallard duck spreads its 8.5-metre wingspan alongside Highway 9. It was built in 1996.

Poplarfield
The 7.3-metre-long whitetail deer was built in 1990.

Off the Beaten Path

Travel a few of Manitoba's secondary highways and there are many more roadside attractions to see.

Altona

A giant easel depicting Van Gogh's Sunflowers was built in 1998. It's one of eight such roadside attractions worldwide, built as part of an international art effort. Sunflowers were chosen as the subject for the Altona easel because the town calls itself the "Sunflower Capital of Canada."

Arden

The town celebrates the provincial flower and the community's annual Crocus Festival with a sculpture of crocuses. The three crocuses each measure a total of 5 metres in height, are located south of town and were built in 2000 as part of a millennium project.

Ashern

The town has hosted an annual international "One Box Sharptail Hunt" for more than 25 years, and for just about that long, a 5-metre-tall sharptail grouse has served as the town's welcoming mascot.

Austin

This town celebrates its farming heritage with an antique tractor perched near the town's official sign.

Boissevain

This town boasts unique two mascots: a big bear, erected near the Irvin Goodon International Wildlife Museum, and Tommy the Turtle, erected in 1974 initially as a salute to the Canadian Turtle Derby. Boissevain didn't host its own turtle derby until 1987, and the event ran until 2001. But not to fret. Tommy the Turtle is not obsolete. Today, the town celebrates the Turtle Island Festival where avid turtle racers can watch a turtle racing demonstration.

Dominion City

This sturgeon sculpture measures 4.7 metres in length, the exact same size as an actual sturgeon pulled from the nearby Roseau River in 1903.

Dunrea
The 567-kilogram statue of a snow goose erected on the south side of town was build as a millennium project.

Elm Creek
For a while, anyhow, the community of Elm Creek thought it had the world's largest fire hydrant when it erected its bright red, 9-metre-tall replica in 2001. It beat out the 7-metre-tall, Dalmatian-spotted hydrant in Beaumont, Texas, for the title. However, it seems the community jumped the gun a little since, just a few short months before, artist Blue Sky erected a near 12-metre version in South Carolina.

Emerson
A life-size sculpture of a Northwest Mounted Police officer on horseback graces the front yard of the information building.

Erickson
A 2-metre-tall Viking ship has graced Main Street's west end since 1983.

Gilbert Plains
Golf Ball Gilbert rolled onto the scene in Gilbert Plains in 1997. The 3.4-metre-tall mascot landed in the centre of town as the community mascot after the oddball design won an "economic development contest." FORE!

Glenboro
Sara the Camel took her stand on the junction of Highways 2 and 5 in 1978. The 7-metre-tall mascot appears to be longingly looking north, where, not far away, Manitoba's "desert" is situated.

Holland
A windmill is, naturally, Holland's mascot.

Komarno
The name of this town is the Ukrainian word for mosquito, so it's little wonder the small community opted for a replica of the giant nuisance as its mascot.

La Baroquerie
Celebrating the town's position as the largest milk-producing centre in Manitoba, La Baroquerie erected Brisette, a 3.6-metre-tall Holstein, as its town mascot in 1983.

La Riviere
Tom the wild turkey was built in 1986 in recognition that the wild turkey was first introduced into Manitoba.

Lundar
A statue of a Canada goose stands proud near Lundar on Highway 6. It was built in 1978.

McCreary
This one proves Manitoba has a landscape worthy of skiing. Alpine Archie, a 5.5-metre-tall, 1360-kilogram, ski-wielding fellow graces the village of McCreary. This statue was built in 1978 for the 1979 Canada Winter Games.

Meleb
Three fibreglass mushrooms are perched atop a stone and concrete foundation. The statue, erected in 1993, pays tribute to three types of mushrooms found in the region: the smorzhi (morel), kozari (boletus) and pidpankay (honey mushroom).

Onanole
The 4.7-metre-tall and 8-metre-long elk is Onanole's mascot and official symbol of the community.

Pinawa
The construction of a sundial was chosen as Pinawa's millennium project. The roadside attraction was built in 2001.

Roland
A giant pumpkin sits just south of Roland on Highway 23. It was built in 1990 as part of the town's centennial project and is a replica of record-size pumpkin grown there in 1977, recorded at 3.7 metres by 3.7 metres.

Roseisle
Three metal roses complete with 224 thorns and 112 leaves have been Roseisle's Main Street attraction since 1991.

Saint Claude
What was once the "World's Largest Smoking Pipe" sits across the grain elevator in St. Claude. It was built to commemorate the area's first white settlers who hailed from the Jura region of France. Since the manufacturing of pipes was the main industry in the area at the time, the pipe was a nice fit as a town mascot. Incidentally, the town's website now calls the roadside attraction the "World's Second-largest Smoking Pipe."

St. Malo
Two whitetail deer statues were erected in the northeast corner of St. Malo in 1990 to commemorate "the only successful deer relocation program in Canada."

St. Rose
A statue of a large white bull stands guard at St. Rose.

St. Rose du Lac
A replica of the Notre Dame de Lourdes Grotto in France was built in St. Rose du Lac between 1955 and 1961. It's located on Highway 276, on the town's southwest corner.

Steinbach
For the town many view as the "automobile capital of Manitoba," the Rolls Royce erected in 1991 is a fitting symbol. Curiously, there doesn't appear to be a Rolls Royce dealership in town at the present time.

YOU'VE GOT TO SEE THIS (CITIES AND MUST-SEE PLACES)

Wide-eyed Wonder

Learning through play wasn't a new concept in 1982 when Linda Isitt and a few friends started brainstorming ways to open a museum specifically designed for children, but this Winnipeg visionary took the idea to a whole new level. Like any other museum, this one would educate visitors, and it would be interactive and fun too! The first incarnation of the Children's Museum opened its doors and welcomed visitors into a converted 90-year-old warehouse in Winnipeg's cultural district in 1986. It was an immediate hit among youngsters and their parents alike, and by 1988, one expansion had already taken place. Today, the Children's Museum, which is now located at The Forks, is housed in another converted building, the former and oldest-surviving train repair facility in the province. It boasts several permanent exhibits, such as the Tree and Me Gallery where youngsters can climb up a re-creation of an over 5-metre-tall oak tree, dress up in animal costumes and listen to the sounds of the nature. Other fun galleries include a space station, a television studio, a train station, a technology corner and a road construction area. Visiting youngsters can play their way to knowledge any day of the week. As a parent, I can tell you there's nothing better to do in Winnipeg on a cold winter's day with a house full of cabin-fevered youngsters than to take a trip to this children's hotspot.

The Winnipeg Zoo

The zoo started out with an idea and a handful of animals in 1904, and within five years, expanded to include 116 animals representing 19 species. Today it is home to countless species from around the world. One of the zoo's longest-standing residents is

Debbie the polar bear. At the grand old age of 40 years, Debbie is the oldest living bear of any kind in the world today, captive or wild. Only two other polar bears have lived longer; one died at 41 years and another at 43. If Debbie lives another four years, she'll be the oldest living polar bear in the species' history.

The Sound of Money

It was built in 1975, and at just under 15,000 square metres, it doesn't really seem all that big when you consider the Royal Canadian Mint in Winnipeg produces all the coins in circulation in Canada. Still, the state-of-the-art technology is so amazing that in 1996 the mint produced a record-breaking 300 million two-dollar coins in just nine months, and inspection units can check 180,000 blanks per hour.

Swinging Sensation

The Capilano Suspension Bridge in Vancouver might draw upwards of 750,000 visitors each year, but swing your way on down to the town of Souris and you're in for a historic experience of mammoth proportions. The bridge, which at 177.4 metres is over 40 metres longer than its BC cousin, was built by Squire Sowden in 1904 to help folks cross the Souris River.

A Prayer for Peace

Located 113 kilometres south of Winnipeg on Highway 10, on the Manitoba and South Dakota border lies a 947-hectare garden like no other. Known as the International Peace Garden, the site began as a simple rock cairn and was inaugurated on July 14, 1932. A plaque on the cairn reads: "To God in His glory we two nations dedicate this garden and pledge ourselves that as long as man shall live we will not take up arms against one another." It is a fitting tribute to the friendship between two nations with the world's longest shared and undefended border. Along with the 150,000 flowers and countless natural shrubs and brushes that, inevitably, provide a home to deer, beaver, game birds and other wildlife, the garden contains a 14-bell chime, a 36.5-metre-tall concrete Peace Tower, a Peace Chapel and other memorials on site.

Recycler Extraordinaire

I first came upon this odd little attraction on a Sunday afternoon drive with my family back in the early 1990s. It was our routine, at the time, to head for rural parts unknown after Sunday church service, and this day we were heading south from Oakville. I can't say I remember what drew us to Treherne. Perhaps there were road signs pointing to the coming attraction, or maybe the road itself just lured us in. Either way, we somehow found ourselves at a rural acreage just outside of the small village, which was tucked away in a corner on Highway 2 near the Manitoba–U.S. border. At this acreage lived a man and a wife with a very unusual hobby. Bob and Dora Cain had been crafting their extensive collection of

glass bottles into a mini village of sorts. It took three years to collect and peel labels off 4000 bottles, (Dora pulled the short straw and got that illustrious job) and two months of working steady before the first structure was completed in 1982. The following year the couple built a church, furnishing its inside with an organ, stained glass windows, a pulpit and pews. That project required 5000 bottles and was such a success it hosted several weddings and church services. In one year alone, the couple tallied about 7000 visitors, and with that kind of traffic the couple, of course, set out to build a bottle bathroom complete with a functional toilet and sink. After that, they added a wishing well, and the bottle village was complete. Bob has since passed away, but folks in Treherne are attempting to keep his unique village alive by moving it to a site in town and continuing Bob's tradition of hosting visitors all summer long.

SMALL-TOWN STORIES

Old Country Heritage

The first settlers to Altona descended from Russian-Ukrainians in the 1870s. The current site of Altona was formally established in 1885, but visitors can still catch a glimpse of the past just 10 kilometres away in the village of Neubergthal, the town's original settlement, which was designated a National Historic Site in 1989.

A Garden of Paradise

Since 2003, Beausejour has claimed the title of being the "coldest American Hemerocallis Society Display Garden on the planet." The development of the garden came about when Beausejour resident Carol Bender visited the Daylily Gardens in Winnipeg. They are beautiful, come in all shapes and sizes and in almost every colour imaginable, but Carol also noted that the plants were hardy, required little water and multiplied well. That meant they were eco-friendly and would look quite wonderful without excessive maintenance. Thinking that they would adapt nicely in one of Beausejour's parks, which had an assortment of raised beds ready for planting, Carol and a group of other community members set out to research the idea. The end result is a 8094-square-metre site boasting 1022 square metres of raised beds that blossom in a symphony of colours from early June until the onslaught of autumn frost. Along with the 400 daylily cultivars, the Beausejour Daylily Gardens also displays 150 iris cultivars, 40 types of peonies and 50 varieties of lily along with prairie hearty fruit trees and, most recently, the recently cultivated dwarf cherry tree from the University of Saskatchewan.

Heralding the First Settlers

Binscarth's museum might not have a collection of prehistoric bones to brag about, but it does have a skull of a now-extinct bison. The Binscarth & District Gordon Orr Memorial Museum also boasts an impressive display of Native artifacts.

Memorable Moment
The village of Bowsman got its name from a surveyor named
J.B. Tyrell. Located in the Swan River Valley just north of the
community of Swan River, J.B. named the new community
after the first man to step out of the boat, also called the
Bowsman. Initially, the name of the river was Bowsman River.

Golden Fields
The City of Brandon, which was incorporated in 1882, is also
known as "the Wheat City."

Painting the Past

Everything you ever wanted to know about the history of
Carman is front and centre for the entire world to see as you
drive through town. Back in the early 1990s, artist Chris Larsen
was contracted to paint a mural back along one entire side of
a building on the town's Main Street. The mural portrays 19 key
moments or people in Carman's history, from a portrait of the
first couple to settle in the area to a threshing crew, highlighting
the importance of agriculture in the community's economy.

All in a Name

The town of Carberry was named after the Carberry Tower in
Scotland. It's a fitting name when you consider the town was
initially highly populated with folks of Scottish descent. In 1991,
43.25 percent of the population listed their ethnic heritage as
Scottish. That number decreased just five years later when only
28.42 considered themselves Scots.

DID YOU KNOW?

The original 1881 site of the community of Cartwright was
actually located just over 3 kilometres north of the present
town. The community moved to its present site in 1885 after
the Canadian Pacific Railway carved its way through the area.

Look Out Below!

What is known as the Clay Banks, located just outside of Cartwright, is the site of one of Manitoba's own buffalo jumps. The Sonata and Besant First Nations hunters would run herds of bison over the cliffs at the now-2500-year-old site, which would either kill or severely maim the animals. They ate the bison meat and used the hide for clothing and the bone for weapons.

DID YOU KNOW?

When the water's low, assorted remains of the S.S. *Alpha*, a steamboat responsible for hauling supplies and passengers along the Red and Assiniboine Rivers, can be seen between Cypress River and Holland. The steamboat ran into trouble when, on April 27, 1885, it hit a sandbar and was so badly damaged that it was unsalvageable.

Manning the Russians

Cranberry Portage has the unique historic distinction of being one of eight communities across Canada's 55th parallel of latitude to play a defensive role for the entire country. Located just south of Flin Flon—which, according to the army intelligence of the day, was considered a possible Russian military target because of its mines and smelters—the community was chosen as a base for the Mid-Canada Line that would act as a back up for the more northern Distant Early Warning System or DEW Line. So, from the late 1950s to the mid 1960s, Cranberry Portage saw the installation of a radar station. The other Manitoba station was RCAF Station Bird, located near the Limestone River.

Heavenly Abode

Clearwater is home to two original churches, each over 100 years old. St. Paul's Anglican Church was built in 1889 and Knox United was built in 1893. Both churches are located in downtown Clearwater.

Claiming One's Name

When Cypress River was founded in the 1880s, it was originally named Littleton after the town's original founders Robert and Nathaniel Little. The town moved 3.2 kilometres east and 1.6 kilometres north of its original site, which is now only marked by a cairn, and was renamed Cypress River. The community's pride in its origins is evident, calling itself the "Best 'Little Town' on the Prairie."

Eyes North

Churchill's claims to fame are many. Officially Manitoba's most northern community, you can only get to the town of about 1000 residents by train or plane. Churchill calls itself the "Polar Bear Capital of the World," and these fascinating and attractive animals, along with the natural beauty of the area, are responsible for the town's biggest industry—ecotourism. Churchill also boasts Canada's only Arctic Sea port.

Fashion Empire

Nygard International is a multinational company with offices in Canada, the U.S., Asia, Mexico and the Bahamas; and the man at its helm once lived in the town of Deloraine, population 1000. Peter Nygard, founder and chairman of the multimillion-dollar fashion empire, spent some of his early youth in Deloraine where his family, who had emigrated from Finland, owned a bakery. Deloraine's Nygard Park flies 206 flags representing 193 countries from around the world, along with Canada's 13 provincial and territorial flags. Deloraine is home to another unique attraction: it has a stone bank vault (one of only two in western Canada).

DID YOU KNOW?

Manitoba's only commercial coalmine was located in Deloraine. The mine started operations in the 1800s, but by the Depression era, the mine was closed down. Today, visitors can check out some of the abandoned mine shafts by picking up an interpretive pamphlet of the area at Deloraine's Information Centre.

Dugald Disaster

The sleepy town of Dugald doesn't typically get much excitement, especially not back in 1947. But on September 1 of that year it made Manitoba history—and not in a good way. The commuter train, the Minaki Camper's Special, was hauling 326 happily exhausted weekenders making their way back from the lakes of eastern Manitoba to their homes in Winnipeg and its surrounding communities. At Dugald, the eastbound train collided with the westbound Super Continental. For whatever reason, mistakes in protocol were made with tragic results. While the crash would have been deadly already, it was made even more so because the Minaki train was pulling a mixture of wooden and steel cars. The resulting fire, which occurred almost on impact, spread quickly to other passenger cars because of the gas tanks beneath the cars and their wooden structure. In the end, between 31 and 40 people died, depending on the source, and all but six bodies were burned beyond recognition and never formally identified. The fatalities were buried in a mass grave, and a memorial was organized by the city of Winnipeg.

Biggest and Best

Along with a mighty big fire hydrant to brag about, folks in the community of Elm Creek have another claim to fame: the second largest meteorite ever found in Canada was discovered in 1997 by Elm Creek area farmer Tom Wood while he was operating a road grater. The newly discovered gem weighed in at just over 8 kilograms, and researchers believe it collided with Earth 10,000 years ago. They also believe it to be a small part of a much larger meteorite weighing approximately 5000 kilograms. The Elm Creek discovery was the 61st of its kind in Canada and the fifth meteorite recovered in Manitoba.

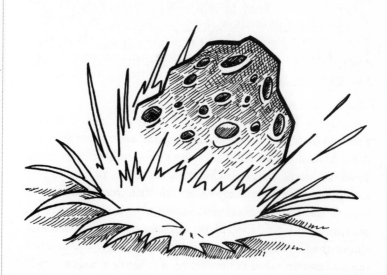

Strange but True

According to one source, there are nine geocaches buried around Elm Creek. For those of you who, like myself before writing this, don't have a clue what a geocache is, I can now tell you that it is a treasure made up of trinkets and such, along with a log book and a pen or pencil, which is buried underground in a weatherproof container along with a Global Positioning System or other type of receiver. Geocaching is something like an outdoor adventure game where folks hunt out these mini treasure chests only to log in their coordinates and leave the bounty behind. According to one source, there are more than 350,000 geocaches in 222 countries. Who knows, maybe the game will spark another reality television series!

Thinking Big

William Fairbanks, who led a group of settlers to the southern border town of Emerson in 1874 with the hope of colonizing the area, must have firmly believed in the power of a name. With a wish and a prayer—and a whole lot of hope for future growth—Fairbanks named the town after the great American poet Ralph Waldo Emerson.

All About Love?

Charles Gonsoulin, an American resident, made headlines in February and March 2005 after attempting to hike from Pembina, North Dakota, to Winnipeg in search of an internet love interest. He was discovered, disoriented and half frozen, by an Emerson RCMP officer near the town's golf course. He couldn't enter Canada legally because of a robbery conviction almost two decades earlier, and his love interest, who lived in Québec, couldn't afford to travel to Los Angeles. The bright move cost the self-employed mechanic all his fingers and many of his toes. It's unknown if he ever met up with his internet hottie.

Out of this World!

He may have been out hunting for precious gems, but Stephen
Michalak found himself national attention instead. It was a cool
day in May 1967, when Stephen set out to Falcon Lake as he
frequently did—nothing out of the ordinary there. The next
day, Stephen found himself a comfortable spot in the woods and
sat down to an early lunch when he noticed a flock of geese
making a whole lot of noise. That's when, according to his state-
ment to the RCMP, he looked up and noticed not one, but two
disc-shaped flying objects. One of the two hovered while the
other landed not 30 metres in front of him. After nearly an
hour, the UFOs took off, but not before expelling a blast of hot
air that burned Stephen's chest and left him incredibly ill. It
wasn't until the following month that officials relocated the site
where Stephen claimed his experience took place. They collected
several soil samples, had them tested and determined there had
been some unexplained radioactivity in the area. The case was
never solved, but it gave Falcon Lake the reputation of being the
site of an honest-to-goodness encounter of the unidentified kind.

Smoking the Fat One

The northern community of Flin Flon garnered considerable attention in 2002 when Prairie Plant Systems Inc., a Saskatoon-based company, established an above-board grow-op when it was granted a four-year contract to produce medicinal marijuana.

Saskatchewan Sister

Flin Flon spans the Manitoba–Saskatchewan border, much like Lloydminister does the Saskatchewan–Alberta border. About 300 of the city's 6200 people live in Flin Flon, Saskatchewan.

A Little Winnipeg

The village of Winnipegosis is named for a Cree word meaning "little muddy water." According to an urban legend, a road in the area was nicknamed "Murder Hill Road" after a 1920s murder occurred there.

DID YOU KNOW?

Flin Flon is so proud of its mascot, Flinty, that in 2003 it commissioned the making of a three-dollar coin with a miner's image on one side and good old Flinty on the other. While the coin is just a collector's item these days, for a year after it was distributed it was considered legal tender within the city.

The Smallest Settlers

While the town of Gilbert Plains was incorporated in 1906, white settlers to the area had made their mark long before then. Myrtle McCurdy was the first white girl born in the area, and Gilbert Clifford Best the first white boy. Both were born in 1900.

Gimli

Gimli is an Icelandic term meaning "heavenly abode." The name was bestowed on the new settlement in October 1875 when Icelandic immigrants first arrived in the area, which had been set aside by the government of the day for a "New Iceland colony."

Historic Landing

On a hot July 23, 1983, folks in Gimli and members of the Winnipeg Sports Car Club were enjoying Family Day activities at the Gimli airport where a car race was taking place on one of the airport's runways. Meanwhile, all was not well in the skies overhead. A Boeing 767 on route to Edmonton from Montréal was experiencing difficulties. A web of miscalculations and computer errors resulted in a plane having inadequate fuel and engines that were shutting down. The only available option was to land the plane, and Gimli's airport was the closest available site. It was nothing short of a miracle that led Captain Robert Pearson, with support from co-pilot Maurice Quintal, to glide the plane to a safe landing—and not a moment too soon. The plane came to a halt just a few hundred feet from where spectators were still gathered for their Family Day events, leaving them and the plane's 61 passengers breathing a deep sigh of relief. It took two days and a million dollars to make the plane flightworthy once again. As of 2007, what has affectionately been nicknamed "The Gimli Glider" was still in service.

DID YOU KNOW?

In just another one of life's little ironies, the mechanics dispatched to Gimli to repair the downed aircraft ran out of gas on route.

Engineering Marvel

Folks who frequently travel through Lockport perhaps don't realize the value of the St. Andrew's lock and dam. The structure, which took 10 years to complete and was officially opened on July 14, 1910, was considered a Canadian engineering marvel and was the first of its kind in all of North America. The lock and dam were built to aid river traffic across the dangerous Lister Rapids, which, prior to that, limited shipping transportation. Its construction opened trading opportunities between the northern and southern parts of the province, attracting people and industry to the area.

Television and Film Debuts

The Avro Arrow is a Canadian aircraft shrouded in mystery, and it's been fodder for at least one television mini-series bearing its name. The 1997 CBC movie *The Arrow*, featuring Dan Akroyd and Christopher Plummer, was partly filmed in Gimli.

The 2002 movie *K-19 The Widowmaker*, starring Harrison Ford, was filmed in the Gimli area, as were parts of the hit new television series *Falcon Beach* and the television series that was sparked by the 1985 Swedish film *My Life as a Dog*.

Motocross Madness

It might be a small town of just 900 people, but Gunthal is home to one of the province's best motocross tracks. Races are held there from July to September.

DID YOU KNOW?

Loosely translated, *gunthal* is German for "green valley."

Lookout!

Blink and you'll likely miss it, but Hollywood must have had its eyes opened long enough to know it liked what it saw. The town of Hartney, population 446, was the site chosen as the setting for the Hollywood film *The Lookout*, staring Jeff Daniels, Joseph Gordon-Levitt and Matthew Goode. Interestingly enough, actress Suzanne Kelley, who plays the character of Nina in the movie, was born in Winnipeg. The movie's release date is some time in 2007.

Northern Oasis

The town of Leaf Rapids was initially built in the 1970s to accommodate workers at the Sherritt Gordon Mines, which opened a copper and zinc mining operation at the nearby Rattan Lake in 1969. But before a single road was ploughed through the pristine northern wilderness, great pains were taken to ensure the areas ecosystems were protected—to this day you need a permit before cutting down any trees in Leaf Rapids. Town planners were also concerned for maintaining the region's heritage, and they paid tribute to the Cree and to the area's wildlife in a visible way by naming all the town streets after an animal and using its Cree name. So instead of Snake Road, it is Kinapik, Wapoose for rabbit, Mikinak for turtle and so on.

DID YOU KNOW?

Aside from being famous for its lock and dam, Lockport is also heralded for having the best hotdogs in the whole doggone country! Skinners Restaurant opened for business in 1929 and served up its first foot-long hotdog for the grand sum of 10 cents. It was doing such a great business that competition in the form of Half Moon Restaurant opened its doors in 1940. Since then, a Sunday drive to Lockport for hotdogs has been a favourite family treat among many Winnipeggers.

Lynn Lake Legacy

Canadian rocker Tom Cochrane was born in the town of Lynn Lake in 1953 and lived there until he was four years old. For several years, Lynn Lake was also the home of comic Lynn Johnston, where she was inspired to create her famous comic strip *For Better or For Worse*.

DID YOU KNOW?

Folks in Kleefeld call themselves Kleefelders.

All That in a Name?

"Melita" wasn't the first name tossed about as a possibility for this southern Manitoba town when, in 1884, a new post office was opening. Folks first suggested "Manchester," since the area was frequently referred to by that name, but it had already been spoken for. One Sunday afternoon, a group of area settlers met to choose a name. The Sunday school lesson that day talked about Paul's shipwreck at Malta (or, as it was then called, Melita). It must have seemed providential, somehow, because everyone agreed that "Melita" would be the perfect name for the new community. Melita was first incorporated as a village in 1902, and at that time an official seal was adopted, along with the town's motto: *Pax et Copia* or "Peace and Plenty."

Hmmmm?

Railway enthusiasts planning to checkout the Miami Railway Museum shouldn't rely on street signs to make their way there. That's because just before Christmas 2005, someone with a whole lot of time on their hands and nothing much to do made off with 44 of them, costing the small town of 500 residents about $7000 for new signs. Of course, these replacement signs have been ordered and most are back in place, but just to be on the safe side you might want a few old-fashioned directions— you know, turn left at the cluster of three trees, that sort of thing.

Salute to the Sioux

If you're not paying careful attention, you could drive right past Minnedosa and not even know it's there. That's because the northern community, named after a Sioux word meaning "flowing water," is snuggled in a deep valley carved into the prairie by the last ice age, making a gigantic pothole. When you're on the highway, it feels like there's nothing around but flat plains until you turn at the directional sign and dip down into town.

For the Fish

A Minnedosa claim to fame is that it is home to the province's longest fish ladder. The 183-metre-long ladder was built by conservationists in an effort to aid fish over the dam in their migration routes. It must be working since sports enthusiasts enjoy fishing on Lake Minnedosa. Incidentally, the lake is also home to the world-class Minnedosa Rowing Centre.

DID YOU  **KNOW?**

The Minnedosa area, and the surrounding pothole region, is considered by Manitoba Conservation as one of the most important breeding areas for canvasback ducks on the continent.

Finding Fossils

The Morden museum is as much an example of evolution as many of its displays. Initially, the town planned a museum that would herald the lives and history of the area's founding settlers. When a huge number of fossilized bones were found in 1972 in a nearby bentamite mine, the museum plans changed focus. Today the museum is known as the Canadian Fossil Discovery Centre and boasts the country's largest collection of marine vertebrates. In the first two years of excavation, 30 mosasaur and 20 plesiosaur specimens were unearthed. "Betsy," a 7-metre-long plesiosaur discovered in 2004 and recovered the following year, is the museum's most recent notable find.

A Few Close Friends

The town of Neelin might be the smallest "town" in Manitoba. According to the 2001 Census, only 10 people call it home. Mysteriously enough, it is home to an experimental research project called the Nuclear Fusion Primary Photon/Electric Exchanger—and it must be as impressive as its name suggests since information on exactly what that is hasn't been made public.

Land of Lillies

Neepawa was named after a Cree word meaning "land of plenty," but these days it could also be called "land of lilies" since the town fathers boast at being the "World Lily Capital." Take a walk through town on a hot summer day and see, around just about every corner, a park or front yard awash with the vibrant colours of dozens of varieties of lilies. Neepawa has earned Manitoba's "Most Beautiful Town Award" more often than any other community.

Almost a Mountain

Pilot Mound was, literally, named after the 35-metre-high mound where it was first located. In 1881, early settlers to the area chose the site and laid out the town in earnest, confident their town would grow into a bustling centre for southern Manitoba. But when the Canadian Pacific Railway laid tracks a mile south, town fathers of the day decided to pull up stakes and move—buildings and all. In 1904, the present-day Pilot Mound was reincorporated, but folks never forgot their roots, referring to the original site as "The Old Mound." Geologists say the blip in the middle of the flat prairie was caused by natural gas activity. Early civilizations living in the area are thought to have revered the site as a "holy hill."

DID YOU KNOW?

Plum Coulee proved to be an unconquerable challenge to bank robber John Krafchenko. Also known as "Bloody Jack" and "Australian Tommy Ryan," Krafchenko met his end following a botched bank robbery on December 3, 1913. In his attempt to rob the town's Bank of Montreal, he killed its manager. Of course, Krafchenko met his maker at the end of a hangman's noose, but not before he posted one last love letter to his secret Plum Coulee love interest. Legend has it she received it the day after he was hanged.

Energy Research

The lake town of Pinawa has seen a few changes in its day. Located on the Winnipeg River, the site was chosen, and the town built for the development of the province's first hydroelectric generating station, but the project was abandoned in 1951 and, of course, the status of the community suffered until 1963. That's when Whiteshell Laboratories (then known as the Whiteshell Nuclear Research Establishment) opened its operations. The facility was built around an organically cooled, heavy water moderated nuclear reactor, the WR-1, which, when it was built in 1963, was the largest of its kind anywhere in the world.

The Name Game

Whether it was because of the trees lining the Plum Coulee creek, or if indeed there was a fabled wanderer named Ivis who happened onto the site 200 years ago and, on the discovery of a plum tree, settled there and announced the area be called Plum Coulee, these days folks in this town celebrate their name with an annual Plum Festival. At one point the town was also known as the sugar beet capital of Manitoba.

One of a Kind

The community of Zhoda is located on Highway 12, and simply had to be included here because its name began with a "Z." How many communities can claim that?

He Shoots—HE SCORES!

Hockey fans might find this tidbit interesting. Poplar Point, a little hamlet on Highway 26 between Portage la Prairie and Winnipeg, is the home of the Hextall family dynasty—or at least a part of this famous hockey family. Patriarch Bryan Hextall was actually born in Grenfell, Saskatchewan, in 1913, but he spent the majority of his youth in Poplar Point, playing hockey there and earning a spot as a member of the Poplar Point Juvenile Team in 1931—the year Poplar Point won the provincials. By 1933, he'd moved on to the Portage Terrier Junior Hockey Team, and by 1934, he was drafted to the Vancouver Lions. Two years later, he moved on to the New York Rangers where he spent the remainder of his career until he retired after the 1947–48 season. His sons, Bryan Jr. and Dennis, as well as his grandson, Ron, all made it into the big leagues. Despite his success and that of his descendants, Bryan Sr. called Poplar Point home until he died in 1984. He was inducted into the NHL Hockey Hall of Fame in 1969 and the Manitoba Sports Hall of Fame & Museum in 1985.

Prize-winning Pumpkin

Roland resident Edgar Van Wyck was recognized, along with his hometown, in the 1977 Guinness Book of Records. His claim to fame was growing giant pumpkins. One source states that the largest pumpkin he'd ever grown weighed in at 560 kilograms. I guess you'd have to see it to believe it!

Cool, Clear, Water

Since 1913, the community of Shoal Lake—located 150 kilometres away in Lake of the Woods—has supplied Winnipeg with its potable water supply. The initial cost for construction of the aqueduct needed to pipe the water into the city was $13.5 million.

Airborne

During World War II, a military airbase was established just on the southern outskirts of Portage la Prairie. For more than 50 years, the community of Southport acted as a training ground for pilots. In 1990, the base closed up shop and the military released the 607 hectares of property to the not-for-profit property management company known as Southport Aerospace Centre Inc. Today the company operates as a business centre featuring aviation and aerospace training facilities, research and development of new products, light manufacturing and educational institutions. The site is also one of the few in North America with its own airport, and it was the first private air traffic control operation to be approved by Transport Canada.

More Than Just Cars

Steinbach seems to be a big draw for folks looking for a more rural setting to put down stakes and raise a family. Based on a 2004 estimate, the town's population is about 10,500 residents. Compared with the two previous census periods, Steinbach has seen an 8.8 percent growth in its population, making it one of the fastest-growing communities in the province.

Building a New Life

The first Ukrainian settlement in western Canada is thought to be Stuartburn. Settlers first migrated to Stuartburn, a small community tucked away in the province's southeastern corner, in the 1890s. As with the founding of any new community, spiritual wellbeing was first and foremost in the minds of these newcomers, and the sod was turned for the building of the Greek Catholic Church of the Holy Ghost in 1898. Many thought this was the first Ukrainian church erected in the western portion of this country. Scholars later discovered it wasn't completed until 1900. That meant the first Ukrainian church built in western Canada, completed in the spring of 1899, was St. Michael's Ukrainian Orthodox Church near Gardenton.

Now You See It

Sundance was founded in the mid 1980s to accommodate employees of the nearby Limestone Dam project. Most of the northern town, which was located near Gillam, consisted of portable buildings. The one-time community pulled up stakes after work on the dam had been completed in 1999, and all the buildings were moved away—including a regulation-size hockey arena. The 4552 square metres of the Sundance Complex were dismantled, packed into transport trucks over a period of about 40 days and moved down south to Pilot Mount. Today, all that remains in Sundance are a few streets and a whole lot of empty lots. The Sundance Complex, on the other hand, has been remade into the Pilot Mound Millennium Recreation Complex that, in addition to the arena, also houses a daycare centre, curling rink, movie and performing arts theatre, fitness centre and more.

Swan Songs

Tucked in the valley between Duck Mountain Provincial Park and the Porcupine Mountains sits the small, agricultural town of Swan River. It's believed the town got its name from the trumpeter swans that once frequented the area. It was officially founded in 1900, but settlers were in the area long before that. It was in Swan River that the Northwest Mounted Police (now the Royal Canadian Mounted Police) band first held a public performance.

Royal Proclamation

Manitoba's largest northern city of Thompson was incorporated as a city in 1970 with the royal family attending the event. At that time the city had a population of about 20,000 residents. Today, the population is closer to 13,256.

Community Resilience

Much of Treherne's history is shrouded in mystery, mostly because of the numerous fires that have destroyed official records. It is known that as early as 1881, the town had a post office, a boarding house and a blacksmith shop. A few years later, in 1886, the railway came through town, and with it several other buildings sprang up. But by 1890, the community faced its first devastating fire, which wiped out an entire block. Not even a decade later, in 1898, another fire destroyed another block. In 1999, another fire destroyed an almost century-old hotel.

War also took its toll on the small prairie community. In World War I alone, 19 men lost their lives in conflict. Another seven fell during World War II. Despite all the hardships over the years, Treherne is almost like the little engine that could. Even with a relatively small population—Treherne is home to about 650 people and the surrounding Rural Municipality of South Norfolk to about 1246 based on 2001 Census figures—the town has a council and mayor, an RCMP detachment, a fully equipped fire station, a Canadian Imperial Bank of Commerce, a credit union and all other necessary amenities and conveniences.

Centre Point

The community of Wabowden is named after W.A. Bowden. From the early 1900s to 1913, the settlement was known as Mile 137 but was renamed after the Federal Department of Railways and Canals chief engineer of the day. Although it's located about 111 kilometres southeast of Thompson in what Manitobans call the northern part of the province, Wabowden is almost the province's exact geographic centre.

Best of the Best

Ask anyone, and chances are you won't find an adult who hasn't heard of the magazine *Reader's Digest*. It's highly unlikely, however, that anyone knows Lila Acheson, one of the magazine's founders, was born in Virden. The year was 1889, a mere seven years after the founding of the community, when little Lila was born to a Presbyterian minister and his wife. Lila was still a youngster when the family moved to the U.S., but there's no doubt about it—this province breeds some pretty amazing folks. In 1922, Lila and her new husband, Wallace DeWitt, decided to launch a magazine that published the best of the best of already published works—an idea that was shot down when pitched to existing publishing empires of the day. Lila and Wallace had the last laugh, however. Their upstart publishing empire has been growing ever since.

By Farmers, For Farmers

A small, rural community of just over 500 people is home to one of North America's leading insurance companies. The Wawanesa Mutual Insurance Company started out as a discussion between two men chatting over an open campfire about the struggles farmers faced back in the summer of 1895. From that, Alonzo Fowler Kempton persuaded 20 farmers to invest $20 each into the idea, and by 1898, an insurance company was born. Today, the company maintains an office in Wawanesa, along with others throughout Canada and the U.S. and remains one of the largest property and casualty insurers in Canada.

Romantic Getaway

As the 10th largest freshwater lake in the world, there is little wonder Lake Winnipeg has long-attracted visitors. From 1900 (when the Canadian Pacific Railway came onto the scene and purchased a parcel of undeveloped land with the intent to build a lakeside community named Winnipeg Beach) to this day, the site attracts waves of weekend visitors year round, and especially throughout the summer months. Its heyday was definitely during the first few decades of the 20th century. The posh new hotels built to accommodate visitors often sported "No Vacancy" signs, especially during long weekends when as many as 40,000 weekenders would descend on the beach. Winnipeg Beach also boasted a 13,000-square-metre dance hall called the Pavilion, which, before it was destroyed by fire in the 1950s, was believed to be the largest dance hall in western Canada.

Winnipeg's proximity to a lake-riddled wilderness draws a considerable portion of its population to the cottage. Perhaps this is what has kept Winnipeg Beach a popular holiday destination, although its ongoing popularity pales in comparison to its early years. Crowds began to thin by the 1950s when folks started travelling to Grand Beach, Victoria Beach or the Whiteshell. By 1964, the CPR had dismantled its on-site amusement park at Winnipeg Beach, which included a wooden roller coaster that was thought to be the largest of its kind in Canada.

DID YOU  KNOW?

Known as the Moonlight Special, tickets on the Canadian Pacific Railway train running beach-bound Winnipeggers to and from Winnipeg Beach on weekends in the early 1900s cost a grand total of 50 cents for a round trip.

Of Hudson Bay Fame

The northern Manitoba community of York Factory is situated about 100 kilometres south-southeast of Churchill on the shores of Hudson Bay. Since the 17th century, it was the site of the historic headquarters of the Hudson Bay Company and remained so until it was closed in 1957. The former company headquarters were in a 1831 wooden building considered the oldest and largest wooden structure in Canada built on permafrost. Today, Parks Canada has assumed responsibility for the landmark, naming it the York Factory National Historic Site of Canada. Aside from summer staff and occasional hunting parties, York Factory is essentially a ghost town.

GHOST TOWNS

Echoes of the Past

The oldest parts of any province are littered with remnants of communities that, though they once pulsated with voices and dreams and ambition, were silenced for one reason or another. Perhaps a new highway was built a few miles away providing better transportation or import and export opportunities. The advent of the railway, of course, spurred on or extinguished potential growth depending on its proximity to whatever community. Poor soil (for farming), lack of an available water source and many other factors worked to determine if a place would survive or wither away into ghost town history. Anywhere you'll find old, dilapidated buildings, chances are you'll hear a neighbourhood tale or two about the ghosts that currently inhabit it. Old, back-country roads and deserted byways are also fodder for such tales. Ask any long-time Petersfield resident about the ghost of Pilatski Road, and you'll hear a tale or two about a distant light that appears from time to time and theories of what unsettled spirit might have caused the phenomenon. (An old boyfriend of mine once filled my young, impressionable head with tales of ghostly apparitions in the area.) City sightings aren't unusual either. Be aware that these reports, as with all such encounters, are not easily verified and could conceivably be little more than legend.

Narcisse No More

The village of Narcisse, once located north of Inwood, exists no longer. It officially lost village status in 2000 after the storeowner closed shop for the last time and moved away. Ten years earlier the Canadian National Railway, which aided in the community's formation in 1914, had removed the last vestiges of track, leaving nothing behind but an overgrown, winding pathway. The community was originally named Bender Hamlet after Jacob Bender, the Jewish businessman who first settled there in 1902. He'd brought 18 families with him from Europe, and by 1917 the community had grown to include 133 people. But the land was poor, and despite all their hard work, the families couldn't make a living there and were forced to move on. Those that remained renamed the community Narcisse, after then president of the Jewish Colonization Association Narcisse Levine. Bender Hamlet, or Narcisse, was one of few Jewish settlements in rural Manitoba. The majority of Manitoba's Jews immigrated to Winnipeg. Today, all that's left behind at the original homestead site are a few abandoned buildings, the old store and a small cemetery.

Gold! Gold!

An example of the power of gossip is no better demonstrated than in the development of the village of Neelin. Located in the Pembina Valley, settlers first came to the area in 1881, but it was the promise of gold in the 1930s that drew residents in far greater numbers. That's happened before, of course, but usually the claims of gold are somewhat substantiated. In the case of Neelin, the claim of gold was nothing more than a joke. Once newcomers learned that the gold wasn't a promise to be realized, homesteaders pinned their hopes on farming and the railway. To be fair, the community thrived somewhat, boasting a school, a store, a grist, a sawmill and several other buildings, but by 1961 the railway had pulled up its tracks, and in 1967 the last store hung its "Closed" sign for the last time. Today, only a few steadfast folks remain in what might otherwise be known as Manitoba's gold town that never was.

Preserving the Past

A historic cairn and a blacksmith museum, in the town's original building, mark the site of the original 1881 community of Cartwright, now known as Old Cartwright. While the present-day town of Cartwright is alive and kicking, its first incarnation is little more than a tiny ghost town with just a few vestiges of yesteryear remaining. Cartwright has made additional efforts at preserving its past with the Boundary Trail Heritage Region, an area set aside for five original historic buildings—Todd's Shoe Repair, a post office, Manitoba Telephone System, the Cartwright School Museum and Badger Creek Museum.

Boom and Bust

Northern Manitoba is home to a gold town that, for a time, delivered at least some of what it promised. Herb Lake Landing was founded on the shores of Wekusko Lake in 1914. Miners and their families flocked to the area, and the community grew into quite a northern hub in its day. But all good things must come to an end; by the late 1950s the mines had closed, and as residents migrated elsewhere, Herb Lake became nothing more than a ghost town. Pictures from the 1960s depict the slow deterioration of the community, and bush has now reclaimed much of the land.

DID YOU KNOW?

While you won't find a lot of people in Narcisse, you will find way more red-sided garter snakes than you'd ever hoped to see in your lifetime. In fact, the entire Interlake region is rife with them, but at this particular site, the Narcisse Wildlife Management Area boasts "the world's largest snake dens." In spring, tens of thousands of snakes emerge from their dens and spend two or three weeks mating. They then disperse until autumn when they return to their dens and prepare for hibernation.

HAUNTINGS

Portage la Prairie

A lovely, blonde lass was at one time reported to be wandering the hallways of the nurses residence in what was once a school of nursing called the Manitoba School.

Selkirk's Haunted Church

This tale frightened me as a youngster in the Anglican church. The cemetery surrounding St. Andrew's on the Red is reportedly haunted by several ghosts. Some people have claimed to have seen a woman in white, others a man in black. Some stories have told of a ghost car and others simply a pair of red, glowing eyes. I even remember tales of people running around the church three times at the stroke of midnight and disappearing forever!

Another Selkirk Spirit

The ghost of a man is said to haunt the basement of a building on Manitoba Avenue. The story goes that he was a homeless man living in the basement and was forced to leave because of impending construction. Distraught because he did not want to leave, he hung himself, but his spirit apparently lives on.

Department Store Ghost

It was eight storeys tall and occupied a square city block, but today, Winnipeg's fabulous Eaton's department store is no more. Demolition of the old building began in 2002 as the city made way for a new arena, MTS Centre. Back when there was still a catalogue department housed there, at least one ghostly presence was believed to inhabit the halls at night. According to one story, a janitor came face to face with an apparition of a woman in black. While he managed to cope with seeing the ghost, when he heard a woman calling his name and no one appeared to be there he was scared silly and left the building, never to return.

Haunted Hotel

The Fort Garry Hotel might be Winnipeg's finest when it comes to overnight accommodations, but it's also one of the city's most famous haunted buildings, and the historic building is a stop on the Haunted Winnipeg ghost tour. Staff and visitors alike have reported seeing more than one ghostly figure, including a mysterious man and a ghostly woman in a white ball gown who move about the hotel.

Eat, Dring and Be Haunted

It's been a long-standing urban legend from as far back as I can remember that Winnipeg's Mother Tucker's Restaurant is haunted. Visitors to the restaurant have reported seeing a face in the bathroom mirror; some say the face is of a man, and others say it's a woman. Either way, the restaurant is located in a former Masonic Temple, built in the 1890s.

The Walker Theatre

Another haunted Winnipeg landmark with several sightings and at least one standard theory behind it is the Walker Theatre. Built in 1906–07, the theatre seats more than 2000 people, and the sound of applause has been said to resonate throughout the building even when it's standing empty. Banging, footsteps and other sounds have also been reported. One theory is that the spooky sounds are made by the spirits of Laurence Irving and Mabel Hackney, who drowned when the *Empress of Ireland* collided with another ocean liner and sank on May 29, 1914. The tragic accident happened just a week after the couple performed at the theatre.

A Neighbourhood Haunting

Winnipeg Sun newspaper reports dated April 26, 2001, recount strange happenings in a north-end Winnipeg home where the family had sought the help of the clergy to exorcise demons. The story explains how a "tortured soul" of some sort had left bruises on the arms and ribs of the lady of the house and caused other havoc. At least one police officer took the couple's claim seriously, reportedly bringing a priest on site to bless the house. In the article, area residents were said to have confirmed the house's seemingly bad karma.

Experiments in Ectoplasm

Although his house was never haunted, while grieving the loss of his son during World War I, a noted Winnipeg doctor started delving into the possibility of afterlife and other psychic phenomenon. From 1918 to 1945, Dr. Thomas Hamilton conducted a wide range of experiments and lectured throughout Europe, the United Kingdom, the United States and Canada on his findings, which included, among other claims, the "proof" of ectoplasm.

COMMUNITY CELEBRATIONS

A Little Ukrainian on the Prairie

With more than 40 percent of Dauphin's 8085 residents claiming Ukrainian heritage, it's no wonder the small city on the prairie hosts Canada's National Ukrainian Festival every August. The event began with little more than a few interested folk, a brainstorming session, a goodwill blessing from Dauphin's Chamber of Commerce, a box of letterhead and five dollars worth of stamps. During the three-day celebration, which takes place during the August long-weekend, festival-goers can take in all types of entertainment such as the Zirka Dance Ensemble, the Canadian National Ukrainian Federation Choir and the Dancing Cossacks & Co. There's also an on-site heritage village and memorial park, ethnic food vendors and workshops highlighting traditional Ukrainian craftsmanship, all against a backdrop of an occasional Cossack cannon. If you love pyrogies, there's no better place to be!

Under the Harvest Moon

Clearwater's claim to festival fame, since 2002, is its annual Harvest Moon Music Festival. As with other harvest festivals, Clearwater's event celebrates the farming community and its effect on rural life, but the town takes the celebration to a more significant level. The festival addresses the importance of getting back to basics by promoting "alternative sustainable agriculture" and serving up healthy helpings of the very best organic cuisine along with music provided by an assortment of prairie musicians. The Harvest Moon Society, which is responsible for organizing the event, also promotes rural living throughout the year with farm and natural tours. It has also established the Centre for Alternative and Sustainable Agriculture (CASA) and the Organic Mentorship Program in a converted elementary school in Clearwater.

DID YOU KNOW?

Based on an economic impact study, Winnipeg's Folk Festival generates more than $16 million for the province and $14 million in Winnipeg.

Music Madness

What began as an addition to Winnipeg's 100th birthday celebration in 1974, attracting 22,000 people to the free event, has catapulted into the annual Winnipeg Folk Music Festival with a $3 million operating budget. Seven stages strategically set up throughout Birds Hill Park, located just north of Winnipeg on Highway 59, accommodate more than 250 artists over a three-day summer weekend. Headliners over the years have included Kenny Rogers, Mike Seeger, Bruce Cockburn, Ricky Lee Jones and the group Austin City Limits—and there's something happening for all age groups and every member of the family. Like any other festival there's a line-up of food vendors and specialty craft vendors, but unlike other festivals this one has a rather unique distinction as the first event of its kind to be certified by Canada's Environmental Choice Program with an EcoLogo as a "green event" in recognition of its efforts to be environmentally proactive.

Festival of the Nations

In the 1960s, social historian John Porter was credited with calling Canada a "vertical mosaic," differentiating it from the U.S. perspective of their country as a melting pot. Porter recognized that Canada was represented by various and distinct ethnic groups, and he pointed out that often a person's ethnic background dictated their success in Canadian society. Whether it's because of Porter's studies on the matter, the publication of his much-revered book *Vertical Mosaic* or the media hype it all produced, since then Canadians have slowly altered their initial narrow outlook and today, we as a nation try to celebrate our diversity.

Winnipeg leads the country when it comes to celebrating this diversity. More than 40 pavilions each feature a different ethnicity with traditional dance, food, clothing, art, libations and the like. Known as Folklorama, the two-week festival, which takes place every August, started out 31 years ago and is primarily a volunteer-run event. Pavilions are set up throughout the city at available school gymnasiums, arenas, community centres, churches and other available venues, and depending on the popularity of any one pavilion, folks could be lined up for city blocks waiting to get in. Winnipeggers who take in the event each year usually plan these two weeks much like they would for a holiday—day one, British pavilion; day two, Ukrainian pavilion; and so on. The event website even offers fairgoers an easy way to customize their itinerary. If Winnipeg's many other attributes haven't put this city on the map, Folklorama surely has.

Corn Cobs and Bobbing for Apples

Morden's first festival might have been held in September 1967, and was initially a Canadian Centennial project, but it wasn't until December 30, 1976, that the festival was first incorporated.

What hasn't changed over the years is that admission to this festival has always been free. The Morden Corn and Apple Festival runs for three days, usually in late August, usually kicking off with the town's annual summer parade and serving up hot buttered corn on the cob and all the apple pie you can eat.

Fur Trade Fame

Down the river you can hear a wind song,
Bearing tales of the voyageur...

St. Boniface is home to a festival that each year celebrates the travellers who, while working for the fur-trading companies of Canada's pioneering years, braved a wild and unforgiving wilderness. Festival du Voyageur screams history like no other festival in the country. Everything about it, from recreating the historic Fort Gibraltar to learning everything you ever wanted to know about making pemmican and bannock, is a celebration of a bygone time and a contribution to life today that simply can't be forgotten. The festival was founded in 1969, and each year it's expected to generate more than $5 million in revenue for the city of Winnipeg and another $6 million for the province.

Exhibition Tradition

Since 1952—and that, as I like to tease my sister who was born that year, was many, many years ago—the Red River Exhibition has been tantalizing Manitobans with the very best in fair attractions. Trust me, I know. Hailing from Winnipeg, or more specifically Transcona, to me the Red River Exhibition represented something akin to a trip to Hawaii. It had the biggest and best Ferris wheels (and I'm not sure I'd ever ridden on one before my visit to the "Ex"), more than its share of obnoxious carnies, and my 1970s introduction to the event was nothing short of a virgin experience since I'd never seen anything like it before. Back then, the exhibition was set up on Winnipeg's west end, near the Assiniboine Downs Race Track, and the entire scene became more elaborate each year. By 1997, the Ex secured a year-round home at that same location, giving it a sense of permanence but in no way reducing the excitement that folks, especially youngsters, feel in anticipation of the actual fair days, which run for about a month, from sometime in June to July.

Velkomin! Welcome!

Saluting people's Icelandic heritage is what the Icelandic Festival of Manitoba is all about, and Gimli has hosted the event since 1932 when the festival moved there from Winnipeg. The festival's history dates back even further to 1890, when it was first held in the windy city, making this (organizers believe) the second oldest continual ethnic festival in North America. Folks can take part in all the typical summer festival fare, along with traditional events such as selecting the Fjallkona (Maid of the Mountain) and the interactive history displays at the Viking Encampment on Harbour Hill Park. The Fris-Nok Tournament is a homegrown game that, from what I can deduce, requires two posts, two empty bottles and a *fris-nok* disc (otherwise known as a Frisbee), and needs to be seen to be understood. The Icelandic Festival is held in early August.

Mush, Mush!

Flin Flon's annual sled dog races are the main draw in the city's Bust the Winter Blues Festival. The event is a cooperative effort between Flin Flon and area and the city's Indian–Métis Friendship Association. There are four categories of races: the ten-dog, six-dog, four-dog junior and the two-dog pro-mutt events. Other traditional pioneering events at the festival include snowshoe racing and log-sawing and nail-pounding competitions. If you have a good sense of humour you'll get a chance to tickle your funny bone with the funniest joke and funniest jigging competitions. The festival, which began in 2003, is usually held in the beginning of February.

Back-40

Another event sure to draw visitors to Morden is the Back Forty Festival. The annual event, which is hosted in June, began in 1989. Its goal is simple: to "Keep Home Made Music Alive." The non-profit group behind the festival, the Back Forty, not only hosts the main music event in June, they also host a music-themed fundraising event in June and are responsible for organizing the Corn & Apple Back Forty Boogie Social in August. Looks like folks in this town can't complain that there's nothing to do in Morden!

Mighty Fine Muscle

I admit it. My only exposure to muscle man competitions is the brief snippets I've seen when flipping through television channels. It appears to be all the rage in some circles, even in smaller communities. In Morden, the Morden Mighty Man competition is held near the town's Friendship Centre during the town's Corn and Apple Festival weekend. Fellas interested in facing the challenge compete in five events: Farmer's Walk (where competitors carry two 82-kilogram cylinders over a specified course); Medley (a timed event); Circle of Pain (where competitors carry a 272-kilogram pole over a designated area); Car Deadlift (two competitors face off against the other, each lifting one end of a Pontiac Grand Am and keeping it suspended in air until one of the two lets go); Tractor Pull (using a hand-over-hand technique for 24 metres. The crowds might get a kick out of watching these exploits, but I'll bet the participants are glad when it's all over. Talk about a workout!

TOP 10 REASONS TO LIVE IN MANITOBA

10. Lonely? Just knock on your neighbour's door, and chances are they'll throw it open and ask you in for a cup of tea—or maybe even dinner! After all, Manitobans take their "friendliest province" status very seriously.

9. Manitoba has the biggest, best, most pristine lakes in the country.

8. There is absolutely no reason to ever be bored. Not only is Winnipeg a mecca of cultural and entertainment opportunities, communities everywhere seem to boast an abundance of activities.

7. You don't pay health care premiums in Manitoba. We take care of our own!

6. There are no mountains, minimal skyscrapers and you can travel in just about any direction of the compass by road. This all equals no need for claustrophobia!

5. If you don't own a hairdryer, don't worry. Just bring a brush and hair mousse and stand on the corner of Portage and Main.

4. No ice in the freezer for your cocktail? If the calendar reads anywhere between September and May, that shouldn't be a problem. Just keep a pail of water out back and chip away!

3. Want to make it to the NHL? You'll have no better training ground than the natural-ice arenas of most small Manitoba towns. Long before the end of the season, the ice is more like slush than a rink, and if you can skate and score on that, nothing will ever stop you!

2. The mosquitoes are so big you can see them coming and hide.

And, finally, the number one reason to live in Manitoba:

1. Snow days!!!

ABOUT THE ILLUSTRATORS

Patrick Hénaff

Born in France, Patrick Hénaff is now based in Edmonton. He is mostly self-taught and is a versatile artist who has explored a variety of media under many different influences. He now uses primarily pen and ink to draw and then processes the images on computer. He is particularly interested in the narrative power of pictures and tries to use them as a way to tell stories, whether he is working on comic pages, posters, illustrations, cartoons or concept art.

Graham Johnson

Graham Johnson is an Edmonton-based illustrator and graphic designer. When he isn't drawing or designing, he...well...he's always drawing or designing! On the off-chance you catch him not doing one of those things, he's probably cooking, playing tennis or poring over other illustrations.

Roger Garcia

Roger Garcia immigrated to Canada from El Salvador at age seven. Because of the language barrier, he had to find a way to communicate with other kids, so he discovered the art of tracing. It wasn't long before he mastered this technique, and by age 14, he was drawing cartoons for the *Edmonton Examiner*. He taught himself to paint and sculpt; then in high school and college, Roger skipped class to hide in the art room and further explore his talent. Roger's work can be seen in a local newspaper and in places around Edmonton.

ABOUT THE AUTHOR

Lisa Wojna

Lisa Wojna, author of several other non-fiction books, has worked in the community newspaper industry as a writer and journalist and has travelled all over Canada, from the windy prairies of Manitoba to northern British Columbia, and even to the wilds of Africa. Although writing and photography have been a central part of her life for as long as she can remember, it's the people behind every story that are her motivation and give her the most fulfillment.